Decolonizing Palestine

Decolonizing Palestine

THE LAND, THE PEOPLE, THE BIBLE

Mitri Raheb

ORBIS BOOKS
Maryknoll, New York 10545

ORBIS BOOKS
Maryknoll, New York 10545

Fathers and Brothers
MARYKNOLL™

Third Printing, March 2024

Founded in 1970, Orbis Books endeavors to publish works that enlighten the mind, nourish the spirit, and challenge the conscience. The publishing arm of the Maryknoll Fathers and Brothers, Orbis seeks to explore the global dimensions of the Christian faith and mission, to invite dialogue with diverse cultures and religious traditions, and to serve the cause of reconciliation and peace. The books published reflect the views of their authors and do not represent the official position of the Maryknoll Society. To learn more about Maryknoll and Orbis Books, please visit our website at www.orbisbooks.com.

Library of Congress Cataloging-in-Publication Data

Names: Raheb, Mitri, author.
Title: Decolonizing Palestine : the land, the people, the Bible / Mitri Raheb.
Description: Maryknoll, NY : Orbis Books, [2023] | Includes bibliographical
   references and index. | Summary: "Develops a decolonial Palestinian
   theology that critiques the settler-colonial project of Israel and its
   Christian theological support"—Provided by publisher.
Identifiers: LCCN 2023007277 (print) | LCCN 2023007278 (ebook) | ISBN
   9781626985490 (trade paperback) | ISBN 9798888660072 (epub)
Subjects: LCSH: Christianity and politics—Palestine. | Christian Zionism.
   | Settler colonialism—Palestine. | Settler colonialism—Israel. |
   Decolonization—Palestine. | Palestine—In the Bible.
Classification: LCC BR115.P7 R2313 2023 (print) | LCC BR115.P7 (ebook) |
   DDC 261.7095694—dc23/eng/20230629
LC record available at https://lccn.loc.gov/2023007277
LC ebook record available at https://lccn.loc.gov/2023007278

To all those who believe in justice
and resist settler colonialism in Palestine and beyond

Contents

Introduction

For Palestinians, including the Palestinian Christian community, Palestine is a real land with real people. It is our homeland, the land of our ancestors. For Christians in the West, Palestine is an imagined land, a land that they know mainly from the Bible. It has little, if anything, to do with the real Palestine.

By "Christians in the West," I am not talking just about evangelical theologians or Christian Zionists. I also mean well-regarded, mainstream, and accomplished theologians of many denominations. Over the last seventy years, many theological concepts have advanced and colonized the minds of generations of theologians worldwide. These concepts may have been well intentioned, but they perpetuate an orientalism that has dangerous implications in the current context of occupied Palestine.

In their naiveté, Christian theologians continue to use language and theological ideas that support current Israeli settler colonialism, causing great harm to the people of Palestine. It is time to decolonize this theology that strips the indigenous Palestinian people of their land, livelihood, and roots. It is time to rupture the theological software that enables Israeli oppression of the people of Palestine. It is time for a paradigm shift, and we must begin with the reality on the ground.

This book is not the theoretical exercise of a theologian living in an ivory tower. The issues at stake in this book pose an existential question to the Palestinian people in general and the Palestinian Christians in particular. This book was born from the intersecting struggles of living as a Palestinian Christian in Bethlehem. As Palestinians, we witness Jewish Israeli settlers colonize our land on a daily basis. A reality experienced by all Palestinians living in historic Palestine, Israeli settler colonialism leaves no room for the next generations of Palestinians as the land around our homes is taken day after day. As Christians, we experience the weaponization of the Bible to drive this colonial project and endow it with a theological grounding. The Bible that is a part of our heritage is being turned against us to enshrine Jewish supremacy and promote the settler colonization of our land.

This book is a first attempt to bring settler colonial theory in dialogue with Palestinian theology. It is an exercise in the further development of a contextual and decolonial Palestinian Christian theology that addresses settler colonial theories. It is a wake-up call for people interested in Israel/Palestine to recognize the reality on the ground, to reflect critically and prophetically on the scripture, and to engage in a new paradigm. It is a wake-up call to perceive how the prevailing exclusive nationalist and expansionist ideologies are disguised in biblical language and motives. My hope is that this new paradigm shift will bring us closer to justice and closer to the spirit of God.

The Little Town . . . A Big Ghetto!

My family has its roots in Bethlehem, the place where I was born and where I still live. Its close proximity to Jerusalem has made it an important commercial, religious, and cultural hub in Palestine since ancient times. As a commercial hub, Bethlehem is a principal asset on the main road between Jerusalem and Hebron. As the birthplace of Jesus Christ, the city is also a key tourist destination in the region. As a meeting point between the fertile terraces to the west and the wilderness with its monasteries to the east, the city is a vital cultural meeting point for farmers, shepherds, and city dwellers.

In the fourth to sixth centuries AD, this area became a magnet and center for monastic life. Within three centuries, over 150 monasteries were established in the Bethlehem wilderness. Besides the Christian monasteries, the Bethlehem wilderness has several Muslim shrines, the best known being Nebi Musa, where, according to Muslim sources, the prophet Moses is buried. Apart from its religious and monastic heritage, the Bethlehem wilderness is a tourist site with enormous potential for wildlife observation, hiking, camping, sky gazing, mountain climbing, desert biking, and quad biking. Yet, the reality today is that 86 percent of the land of Bethlehem Governorate is under exclusive Israeli control, whether that of Israeli colonies or by the Israeli military. Only 14 percent of Bethlehem Governorate is currently under Palestinian control. There is no land left for the native people of Bethlehem and the surrounding villages to start new neighborhoods. Under these circumstances, the use of the word *occupation* to explain what is happening in Palestine under the Israeli government does not accurately reflect the process of colonization and the aggressive expansion of settlements on Palestinian land throughout historic Palestine. These colonies are illegal under international law and constitute a human rights violation.

The Bethlehem Governorate covers an area of 254 square miles (658 square kilometers) and has a Palestinian population of about 230,000 people. Israel occupied the West Bank in June 1967, when I was five years old. During the past fifty-five years, Jewish settlers have been intent on strangling our town by surrounding it with Israeli colonies (settlements). Starting in the early seventies, Israel embarked on the construction of exclusive Jewish colonies on land belonging to Bethlehem Governorate. Today there are twenty-seven colonies with close to 150,000 Jewish settlers. The Israeli colonies are developed by private Israeli companies and real estate brokers on prime Palestinian land. Jewish settlers with a Western mind-set are intent on grabbing and exploiting Palestinian land to transform it for exclusively Jewish life and recreation. Investment in these colonies reaches into the billions of dollars and often has financial ties to American moguls like Irving Moskowitz and Sheldon Adelson. The so-called Gush Etzion bloc, for example, strangles the Bethlehem quadrangle with over twenty Jewish colonies, including Gilo and Jabal Abu Gneim (Har Homa) in the north with close to seventy thousand settlers, several colonies around the Betar Illit colony in the west with its sixty thousand settlers, and Efrat and Tekoa to the south and southeast with eleven thousand and four thousand settlers, respectively.

The organization and location of the regional council named the Gush Etzion bloc was not a matter of chance but a deliberate choice. First, their proximity to the Green Line actively expands the area of the State of Israel by encroaching deep into West Bank territory. Second, most of these colonies are built on the western slope of the mountain range that runs from Jerusalem to Hebron with an altitude of 2,500 feet (750+ meters) above sea level, an area with enough annual rainfall to ensure very fertile ground. It is no coincidence that the Bible calls this area of Bethlehem *Ephrata*, meaning fertile ground (Micah 5:2). The Jewish colonies surrounding Bethlehem and its neighboring towns (Beit Sahour, Beit Jala, and Doha) are spread out to encompass the maximum amount of Palestinian land for future expansion, while choking Palestinian towns and making it impossible for them to grow. Most of these colonies are separated from the Bethlehem quadrangle by a nearly thirty-five-mile-long (fifty-six-kilometer), twenty-seven-foot-high (eight-meter) concrete wall, two-thirds of which has been completed, built entirely on occupied land inside the borders of Bethlehem Governorate, making Bethlehem the second-most-affected city by the separation wall.

The second group of Jewish colonies in Bethlehem Governorate was built along the Dead Sea shore and organized within Megilot Regional Council. It comprises seven small colonies with fewer than three thousand settlers. Although small in size, these strategic colonies control nearly twenty miles of Dead Sea coastline, the longest strip on the west of the Dead Sea. When tourists float in the Dead Sea, they seldom recognize that they are floating in water that belongs to Bethlehem but is exploited by a Jewish colony. The Dead Sea, a major tourist attraction and important source of foreign currency through international and domestic tourism, is a rich reservoir of minerals and potash. It is a unique, priceless cultural heritage, and an environmental, therapeutic, and touristic treasure. Along the Dead Sea, there are other attractions, including several freshwater springs: Ein-Faschcha, Ein el-Ghuwer, and Ein et-Turabe. These used to be popular locations for leisure, picnics, and swimming for West Bank Palestinians. During my school years, this was a popular area for outings and picnics, and we loved to swim in the freshwater pools.

Today, this same area is controlled and managed by an Israeli colony that offers recreation to Israeli soldiers and military personnel while access for Palestinians is restricted. The area along the Dead Sea shore makes up around 10 percent of Bethlehem Governorate. The east of Bethlehem Governorate borders Jordan, and Bethlehem should control the western shore and water of the Dead Sea while Jordan controls the eastern shores and waters. Yet Israeli military and settlers control the whole western Dead Sea shore with its mineral deposits, in addition to the water resources that belong to Bethlehem.

In addition to the two settlement blocs discussed above, a third area located to the west of the Dead Sea and east of Bethlehem is currently designated as a military zone and is used by Israel for military training. This three-mile strip in the Bethlehem wilderness runs from north to south, across Bethlehem Governorate, and makes up 40 percent of the land of Bethlehem Governorate. Although called a wilderness, it sits over a good portion of the Eastern Basin Aquifer with nearly 4.5 billion cubic feet of freshwater and is also an important habitat for wildlife. The wildlife and biodiversity of this area are of utmost importance.

This colonization process has been in practice for over a century, since European Jews started their first Jewish settlement in Palestine at the end of the nineteenth century. In 1947, the Jewish population of Palestine owned only about 5 percent of the land. In the 1948 War, Israel took over 77 percent of historic Palestine and pushed over 750,000 Palestinians off their land. Palestinian property was seized, and 86 percent of the land taken was declared state or "absentee" land for use exclusively by Israeli Jews. This policy resembles the Doctrine of Discovery used in other settler colonial contexts. Palestinians were left with 6 percent of the land inside the Green Line, the border set by the Armistice Agreements of 1949. In 1967, Israel occupied the West Bank and Gaza Strip, in addition to the Golan Heights and the Sinai. Land colonization has been ongoing in the West Bank since 1967, and over half of the area is currently under Israeli military and/or settler control. In violation of international law and the Geneva Convention, Israel has invested heavily in building and subsidizing Israeli colonies, transferring over 800,000 Jewish settlers into the Palestinian territory, thereby altering the demography of the West Bank. Today, Palestine resembles a slice of Swiss cheese in which Israel has the cheese, that is, the land and the resources, while the Arab Palestinian population is pushed into the holes in overcrowded towns with no resources. Bethlehem, my hometown, is just one example of this settler colonial policy.

The settler colonial nature of the State of Israel is obvious, and the reality on the ground is crystal clear. The situation is not "complicated" as some claim in order to blur the issue. International law is decisive on this issue, as the many UN resolutions testify. Yet, biblical passages and terms such as "divine rights," "land promise," "Judea," and "chosen people" are constantly repeated to bestow the colonization of Palestine with biblical legitimacy and thus political legality. This terminology is used in church circles, popular events, as well at the highest political levels like the UN Security Council.

The Hebrew Bible: Israel's Last Resort?

On December 23, 2016, the UN Security Council met to discuss the expansion of Israeli colonization of Palestinian land in the West Bank and East Jerusalem. Resolution 2334 (2016) was adopted by fourteen countries with one abstention by the United States under the Obama administration. The resolution reaffirmed the Security Council's stance that Israeli settlements have no legal validity and constitute a flagrant violation of international law. The text reads as follows:

The Security Council,

Reaffirming its relevant resolutions . . .

Guided by the purposes and principles of the Charter of the United Nations, and reaffirming, inter alia, the inadmissibility of the acquisition of territory by force,

Reaffirming the obligation of Israel, the occupying Power, to abide scrupulously by its legal obligations and responsibilities under the Fourth Geneva Convention relative to the Protection of Civilian Persons in Time of War, of 12 August 1949, and recalling the advisory opinion rendered on 9 July 2004 by the International Court of Justice,

Condemning all measures aimed at altering the demographic composition, character and status of the Palestinian Territory occupied since 1967, including East Jerusalem, including, inter alia, the construction and expansion of settlements, transfer of Israeli settlers, confiscation of land, demolition of homes and displacement of Palestinian civilians, in violation of international humanitarian law and relevant resolutions,

Expressing grave concern that continuing Israeli settlement activities are dangerously imperiling the viability of the two-State solution based on the 1967 lines.

The US representative explained that the decision to abstain rather than veto was because settlements undermine Israel's security and erode the prospect of a two-state solution, thereby putting the peace and stability of the area at risk. Once all fifteen Security Council members had been given the floor, Danny Danon, the Israeli representative to the United Nations, addressed the Council:

Mr. President, today is a bad day for this Council . . . This Council wasted valuable time and efforts condemning the democratic state of Israel for building homes in the historic homeland for the Jewish people. We have presented the truth time and again for this Council and implore you not to believe the lies presented in this resolution. I ask each and every Council member who voted for this resolution: Who gave you the right to issue such a decree denying our eternal rights in Jerusalem? . . . We overcame those decrees during the time of the Maccabees and we will overcome this evil decree today. We have full confidence in the justice of our cause and in the righteousness of our path. We will continue to be a democratic state based on the rule of law and full civil and human rights for all our citizens, and we will continue to be a Jewish state. Proudly live and reclaiming the land of our forefathers, where the Maccabees fought their oppressors and King David ruled from Jerusalem.

Just before ending his speech, something happened that captured my full attention. Mr. Danon pulled out a Hebrew Bible, lifted it up, and said, "This holy book, the Bible, contains 3,000 years of history of the Jewish people in the Land of Israel. No one, no one can change this history."

This is the contemporary context of the land of Palestine. The biblical story is used as history in support of a settler colonial project. Specific biblical figures are evoked to legitimize an exclusivist ideology of modern state structure. The Bible is used today by the current Israeli government, by the Zionist movement, and by Christian Zionists to colonize Palestine and to replace the indigenous people by pushing them, slowly but surely, out of the country. Critically for this book, as well as the Christian Zionists, many liberal theologians produce theological literature without context that provides, whether consciously or subconsciously, ideological cover for the colonization of Palestine.

The Structure of the Book

This book comprises four chapters. The first chapter analyzes the past one hundred years of the history of Palestine through the lens of settler colonialism, with emphasis on the interplay between religion and politics. It prepares the ground to understand the Palestinian issue not as a conflict between two parties but as a deliberate and continuous settler colonial project where the Bible is weaponized and the international community is complicit.

The second chapter attempts to provide a new definition of the phenomenon of Christian Zionism, with emphasis on actions rather than beliefs. I argue that Christian Zionism should be defined as a Christian lobby that supports the Jewish settler colonialism of Palestinian land by using biblical/theological constructs within a metanarrative while taking glocal considerations into account.

The third chapter attends to the theme of land and its exploitation in the service of settler colonialism while introducing a decolonial Palestinian reading of the biblical land issue.

The fourth chapter looks at the notion of biblical election and chosen people, a theology that constitutes a theological dilemma for the Palestinian people. While the original context of chosenness was a feeling of powerlessness in the face of empire, chosenness today must be sited within the context of European nationalism, settler colonialism, and American exceptionalism. The chapter concludes with a Palestinian decolonial perspective on the notion of election and chosenness.

The book concludes with an epilogue that analyzes the complicity of the church and politics in support of the Israeli settler colonial project in Palestine. This is one of the last anticolonial struggles in an era largely regarded as postcolonial. Decolonizing Christian theology regarding the Palestinian land and its people is an urgent necessity. The time for a new paradigm is now.

1

Settler Colonialism, Palestine, and the Bible

To best explain the prevailing situation in Palestine, people refer to it as a "conflict": a conflict between two parties, even if they are not equal, a conflict over land and resources, a conflict over holy places deeply connected to identity, or even a conflict between colonizer and colonized. This is the prevailing paradigm used in the media, in academia, and in popular debate. This paradigm is dominant today in describing the current situation as a conflict between Israel and Hamas. Based on this assumption, the international community tries to solve the "conflict," or at least to manage it, yet with no success. Flawed assumptions have led to the deteriorating situation and disastrous outcome to which we are witnesses today.

The framework of "conflict" is misleading to say the least. Even the description of the situation as occupation is inaccurate because, despite Palestine's history, the situation over the past one hundred years cannot be described as occupation. There is a dire need for a new framework and a paradigm shift. This chapter argues that the situation prevailing in Palestine since the Balfour Declaration is one of settler colonialism.

Settler Colonialism

Settler colonialism is a distinct form of colonization that, while existing in practice for centuries, has received increased attention in anthropology and indigenous studies scholarship following the Cold War. Contrary to postcolonial contexts, settler colonialism describes contexts where colonization constitutes an ongoing reality rather than a singular event in the past. Patrick Wolfe and Lorenzo Veracini contributed foundational scholarship in the field that now spans multiple publications underlining the global reach of settler colonialism from Australia to Canada, from the United States to South Africa, from Fiji to Palestine.

The concept of settler colonialism was formulated by Patrick Wolfe in his groundbreaking monograph, *Settler Colonialism and the Transformation of Anthropology: The Politics and Poetics of an Ethnographic Event*, published in 1998. Wolfe set the theoretical framework for the discipline of settler colonial studies.[1] It was followed in 2010 by another comprehensive work by Lorenzo Veracini entitled *Settler Colonialism: A Theoretical Overview*, which emphasized the present global dimension of settler colonialism.[2] The first two decades of the twenty-first century saw a growing interest in this field manifested by multiple publications underlining the global reach of settler colonialism, which stretches from Australia to Canada, from the United States to South Africa, and from Fiji to Palestine.[3]

---

[1] Patrick Wolfe, *Settler Colonialism and the Transformation of Anthropology: The Politics and Poetics of an Ethnographic Event* (London: Continuum, 1999), 52.

[2] L. Veracini, *Settler Colonialism: A Theoretical Overview* (Houndmills, Basingstoke, UK: Palgrave Macmillan, 2010).

[3] F. Bateman and L. Pilkington, eds., *Studies in Settler Colonialism: Politics, Identity and Culture* (Houndmills, Basingstoke, UK: Palgrave Macmillan, 2011); Caroline Elkins and Susan Pedersen, eds., *Settler Colonialism in the Twentieth Century: Projects, Practices, Legacies* (New York: Routledge, 2005); Stuart Banner,

The permanent settlement of colonists in an occupied land is the main feature that distinguishes settler colonialism from classical or neocolonialism. The settler colonialists establish and enforce state sovereignty and juridical control over the indigenous land, ultimately aiming to eliminate the native people. The natives become extraneous while the settlers are cast as natives through different political mechanisms, ideological constructs, and social narratives. The indigenous land is described as *terra nullius,* empty or barren land that is just waiting to be discovered, thus becoming the private property of the settlers. The native people are depicted with racist constructs as savage, violent terrorists, while the settlers are portrayed as the civilized and brave pioneers. To defend the settled property from the savage, a police state is created and is granted extraordinary power over the native people, including power over their civil affairs.

While settler colonialism theory was first used for contexts like Australia, New Zealand, and North America, several major writers have published works recently applying settler colonialism to the State of Israel, among them Lorenzo Veracini, Magid Shihadeh, Steven Salaita, Shira Robinson, Elia Zureik, Nadim Rouhana, Areej Sabbagh-Khoury, Nahla Abdo, and, most recently, Rashid Khalidi in his comprehensive work, *The Hundred Years' War on Palestine: A History of Settler Colonialism and Resistance, 1917–2017.*[4] The majority of Palestinian scholars

---

Possessing the Pacific: Land, Settlers, and Indigenous People from Australia to Alaska (Cambridge, MA: Harvard University Press, 2007); Tracey Banivanua Mar and P. Edmonds, eds., *Making Settler Colonial Space: Perspectives on Race, Place and Identity* (Houndmills, Basingstoke, UK: Palgrave Macmillan, 2010).

[4]Lorenzo Veracini, *Israel and Settler Society* (London: Pluto Press, 2006); Lorenzo Veracini, "The Other Shift: Settler Colonialism, Israel, and the Occupation," *Journal of Palestine Studies* 42, no. 2 (2013): 26–42, https://doi.org/10.1525/jps.2013.42.2.26; Lorenzo Veracini, "What Can Settler Colonial Studies Offer to an Interpretation of the Conflict in Israel–Palestine?," *Settler Colonial Studies* 5,

who applied the paradigm of settler colonialism to Israel were Palestinians from inside the Green Line.[5] However, none of the scholars were trained in theology, nor did they attempt to examine the interplay between settler colonialism and theology. Settler colonialism as a discipline was absent from theological discourse until Finnish Old Testament scholar Pekka Pitkänen's recent study of the books of the Pentateuch and Joshua, referencing the Israeli–Palestinian context.[6] Pitkänen convincingly showed how the first six books of the Old Testament include all of the important features of settler colonialism. In the next section, I apply the settler colonial theory to Israel–Palestine

no. 3 (2015): 268–71, https://doi.org/10.1080/2201473X.2015.1036391; Magid Shihade, "Settler Colonialism and Conflict: The Israeli State and Its Palestinian Subjects," *Settler Colonial Studies* 2, no. 1 (2012), 123; Steven Salaita, *Holy Land in Transit: Colonialism and the Quest for Canaan* (Syracuse, NY: Syracuse University Press, 2006); Steven Salaita, *Inter/Nationalism: Decolonizing Native America and Palestine*, 3rd ed. (Minneapolis: University of Minnesota Press, 2016); Shira N. Robinson, *Citizen Strangers: Palestinians and the Birth of Israel's Liberal Settler State*, (Stanford, CA: Stanford University Press, 2013); Elia Zureik, *Israel's Colonial Project in Palestine: Brutal Pursuit* (London: Routledge, 2015); Nadim N. Rouhana and Areej Sabbagh-Khoury, "Settler-Colonial Citizenship: Conceptualizing the Relationship between Israel and Its Palestinian Citizens," *Settler Colonial Studies* 5, no. 3 (2015): 205–25; Nahla Abdo and Nira Yuval-Davis, "Palestine, Israel and the Zionist Settler Project," in *Unsettling Settler Societies: Articulations of Gender, Race, Ethnicity and Class*, ed. Daiva K. Stasiulis and Nira Yuval-Davis (London: SAGE Publications, 1995), 291–321; Rashid Khalidi, *The Hundred Years' War on Palestine: A History of Settler Colonialism and Resistance, 1917–2017* (New York: Metropolitan Books, 2020).

[5]Areej Sabbagh-Khoury, "Tracing Settler Colonialism: A Genealogy of a Paradigm in the Sociology of Knowledge Production in Israel," *Politics & Society* 50, no. 1 (2022): 44–83.

[6]Pekka Pitkänen, "Pentateuch–Joshua: A Settler-Colonial Document of a Supplanting Society," *Settler Colonial Studies* 4, no. 3 (2014): 245–76, https://doi.org/10.1080/2201473X.2013.842626; see also Pekka Pitkänen, "Settler Colonialism in Ancient Israel," https://www.academia.edu/31712835/Settler_Colonialism_in_Ancient_Israel; Pekka Pitkänen, "Reading Genesis–Joshua as a Unified Document from an Early Date: A Settler Colonial Perspective," *Biblical Theology Bulletin*, February 3, 2015, https://doi.org/10.1177/0146107914564822; Pekka Pitkänen, "Ancient Israel and Settler Colonialism," *Settler Colonial Studies* 4, no. 1 (2014): 64–81, https://doi.org/10.1080/2201473X.2013.812944.

by looking at the historical development of the Jewish settler colonial project from the British Empire to the current Trump era, and the role played by Christian theology in this history.

The Theopolitics of Settler Colonialism: The Case of Israel

Christian theology has played a role in almost all settler colonial projects, including North America, South Africa, and Australia. In his book *Missionary Conquest: The Gospel and Native American Cultural Genocide,* George Tinker, a Native American Lutheran theologian, argued,

> Europe's colonial conquest of the Americas was largely fought on two separate but symbiotically related fronts. One front was relatively open and explicit; it involved the political and military strategy that drove peoples from their land to make room for the more "civilized" conqueror and worked to deprive Indian peoples of any continuing self-governance or self-determination. The second front, which was just as decisive in the conquest if more subtle and less explicitly apparent, was the religious strategy pursued by missionaries of all denominations . . . In this conquest, as in the European conquest of Indian peoples, theology becomes a crucial ingredient, and missionaries become an important strategic phalanx.[7]

What is true for the Americas is true for Palestine. Palestine is not an exception; yet Palestine continues to be the exception. While no one would dare today to cite the Bible to justify settler

---

[7]George E. Tinker, *Missionary Conquest: The Gospel and Native American Cultural Genocide* (Minneapolis: Fortress Press, 1993), 120.

colonialism in Australia or North America, many Christians and Jews have been doing exactly this for nearly two hundred years, continuing to do so this very day in Palestine. Furthermore, the interplay between the settler colonial project in Palestine and biblical interpretation has never been static, undergoing several adjustments amid changing contexts. Here, I highlight five key stages of the relationship between the Jewish Israeli settler colonial project and the Bible.

First Stage: Seeding the Seeds

A renewed interest in Jews and Judaism developed as a result of the religious revival in Europe and the "Second Great Awakening" in the United States during the nineteenth century. The rapid social and political changes of that time made people feel that the second coming of Christ was drawing near. Yet, three developments were a prerequisite for that to happen: the triumph of Protestantism through mission, the defeat of Islam represented by the collapse of the Ottoman Empire, and the conversion of the Jews to Christianity. John Nelson Darby (1800–82), an Anglo-Irish Bible teacher, connected the conversion of the Jews with the restoration of what he called "the Kingdom of Israel" that he saw prophesied in the Bible. His convictions were referenced in the Scofield Reference Bible that became a popular version in that era.

Originally a theological construct, Darby's "the Kingdom of Israel" started to take shape in real politics after the occupation of Palestine by Ibrahim Pasha in 1831. Ibrahim's father, Muhammad Ali Pasha (1769–1849), an Ottoman Albanian, seized power over Egypt after the withdrawal of Napoleon. His dream was to create a modern state based on a European model that would cover the area between the Nile and the Euphrates. Toward that goal, his son Ibrahim Pasha occupied large parts of Syria, including Palestine. During his reign, a British consulate opened and ground was broken for Christ Church, a Zionist Anglican congregation for Jewish converts in Jerusalem, both at Jaffa Gate. This occupation of Palestine by Ibrahim Pasha presented a threat not only to the Ottoman rulers but also to Europeans whose interests in the Middle East were crucial. In order to ensure control of trade routes and resources in 1840, Britain and Austria decided to come to the aid of the Ottomans against Ibrahim Pasha and were successful in pushing him back from Syria and Palestine. A decade later, in the context of the Crimean War (1853–56) in which France and Russia fought for control of the holy sites, an evangelical Christian, the Seventh Earl of Shaftesbury, wanted to know who would obtain the rights over the Holy Land: Palestine and Syria.

Evangelical Christians initially concentrated on the "restoration" of the Jewish people to what was regarded as their ancient homeland: Palestine. Situating the intruders as natives belonging to the colonized land is another feature of settler colonialism. Sending British Jews to Palestine not only served British imperial interests, but it would, in the unspoken hope of British politicians, solve the Jewish question at home. With shrinking space for Jews in Europe, the Zionist movement gradually adopted this particular Christian view of history and its use of biblical prophecy to escape Europe, thereby translating Zionism into a "real political" agenda. In his 1896 publication, *Der Juden Staat,* Theodor Herzl adopted this Anglo-European plan. He argued for a Jewish nation-state as an outpost of Western civilization. Within this state, British Jews could be the managers and Eastern European Jews would provide the cheap labor to develop Palestine.[8] His settler colonial intentions were made crystal clear in his diary in 1895:

---

[8]Theodor Herzl, *The Jewish State: An Attempt at a Modern Solution of the Jewish Question,* ed. Jacob de Haas, trans. Sylvie d'Avigdor (Dumfries and Galloway: Anodos Books, 2018).

We must expropriate gently the private property on the estates assigned to us. We shall try to spirit the penniless population across the border by procuring employment for it in the transit countries, while denying it employment in our own country. The property owners will come over to our side. Both the process of expropriation and the removal of the poor must be carried out discreetly and circumspectly.[9]

The outcome of the First World War gave the movement its worked-for breakthrough. On November 2, 1917, the First Earl of Balfour, Arthur James Balfour, the British Foreign Secretary, wrote to his colleague in Parliament and the prominent British Jewish banker, Baron Walter Rothschild (1868–1937):

I have much pleasure in conveying to you, on behalf of His Majesty's Government, the following declaration of sympathy with Jewish Zionist aspirations which has been submitted to, and approved by, the Cabinet: His Majesty's Government view with favour the establishment in Palestine of a national home for the Jewish people, and will use their best endeavours to facilitate the achievement of this objective, it being clearly understood that nothing shall be done which may prejudice the civil and religious rights of existing non-Jewish communities in Palestine, or the rights and political status enjoyed by Jews in any other country.[10]

[9]Theodor Herzl, *The Complete Diaries of Theodor Herzl*, ed. Raphael Patai, trans. Harry Zohn (Herzl Press, 1960), 88–89.

[10]Rashid Khalidi, *British Policy towards Syria & Palestine, 1906–1914: A Study of the Antecedents of the Hussein-McMahon Correspondence, the Sykes-Picot Agreement, and the Balfour Declaration* (London: Published for the Middle East Centre, St. Antony's College, Oxford, by Ithaca Press, 1980).

The timing of this English Cabinet decision was not by chance. The British army, stationed in Egypt, was ready to storm southern Palestine. On November 22, just a few weeks after the Balfour Declaration, Jerusalem was occupied by the commander in chief of the Egyptian Expeditionary Force, Sir Edmund Allenby. The "biblical promise" of "land" now became the imperial promise of Palestine to the European Jews. The native inhabitants, Christians and Muslims who made up 95 percent of the population, were portrayed negatively as "non-Jewish communities" who might have "civil and religious rights" but no national rights or sovereignty over the land. Distinguishing between civil and religious rights and recognition of national or sovereign governance constitutes another important feature of settler colonialism.

The Balfour Declaration paved the way for Britain's Mandate over Palestine in 1920, with the goal of preparing Palestine for takeover by European Jews. The British Mandate government facilitated the immigration and settlement of European Jews in Palestine, especially after 1933. Palestinian intellectuals like the editor of the *al-Karmel* newspaper, Najib Nassar, the Jerusalemite Ruhi al-Khaldi, and the anthropologist and medical doctor Tawfiq Canaan, to name a few, understood very early on the settler colonial nature of the Zionist movement.[11] The resulting, long political strike in 1936 was a Palestinian revolt against the settler colonial policies of the British Mandate government.

---

[11] Emanuel Beška, "Anti-Zionist Journalistic Works of Najīb Al-Khūrī Nassār in the Newspaper Al-Karmal in 1914," *Asian and African Studies* 20 (2011): 167–92; Emanuel Beška, "Political Opposition to Zionism in Palestine and Greater Syria: 1910–1911 as a Turning Point," *Jerusalem Quarterly* 59 (2014): 54–67; Emanuel Beška, "The Anti-Zionist Attitudes and Activities of Ruhi al-Khalidi," in *Arabic and Islamic Studies in Honour of Ján Pauliny,* ed. Zuzana Gažáková and Jaroslav Drobný (Bratislava: Comenius University in Bratislava, 2016), 181–203; Tawfiq Kanʿān, *Tawfiq Canaan: An Autobiography,* ed. Mitri Raheb (Bethlehem: Diyar, 2020).

Second Stage: Taking the Land

On May 15, 1948, Britain withdrew its forces from Palestine. The European Jews who had been "mapping" the land
for two decades were prepared to take over, and, on that very
same day, they declared the State of Israel, a declaration that
resulted in an attack by Arab forces. The Arab-Israeli War of
1948 gave a major push to the settler colonial project, as 77
percent of historic Palestine was occupied by Israeli troops and
Jewish terror organizations, becoming the State of Israel. A total
of 452 Palestinian villages were destroyed, and over 750,000
Palestinians were driven out of their homes, becoming instantly
displaced refugees.

Eliminating the indigenous population, conquering their
land, and destroying their villages to make the land *terra nullius* are defining features of settler colonialism. Palestinians
underwent a forced migration, compelled to leave their land
and start an indefinite reality as refugees stranded in camps
and in the diaspora. This defeat was coined in the Palestinian
collective memory as the *Nakba*, "the catastrophe." The *Nakba*
created favorable conditions for Israel to proceed with its settler
colonial project through the ethnic cleansing of the indigenous
Palestinian population, the confiscation of their properties
through absentee laws, and putting the remaining land under
military control.

The Palestinian *Nakba* occurred in the context of two important developments related to World War II; developments
that proved crucial for the future of the Israeli settler colonial
project. First, in 1944, US President Roosevelt signed a G.I. bill,
declaring Jews (and Irish and Italian Catholics) to be White and
eligible for compensation. Native and African Americans were
excluded. While for decades Jews in Europe had been considered
different and inferior to White Europeans, American Jews were

now part of the White race.[12] Second, following the US entry into WWII, the phrase "Judeo-Christian tradition"[13] became popular in American culture. Citing K. Healan Gaston, James Loeffler notes that,

> As Americans tried to make sense of their country's role in repelling the Nazi assault on Western civilization, the intertwining of religion and democracy provided a helpful means for Jewish and Christian clergy and politicians to signal their shared commitment to anti-fascism. But its heyday would really arrive only at the war's end as the rhetoric morphed easily into the new vocabulary of Cold War politics. Anti-communist liberals found in the phrase a convenient shorthand "for religious pluralism in general, identifying unbounded diversity and unfettered freedom of belief as the keynotes of democratic life."[14]

However, the creation of a new state with an ancient biblical name caused considerable confusion. Huge efforts were exerted by the State of Israel and Jewish organizations to brand this new State of Israel a "biblical entity," with Jewish migration to Palestine a miraculous "return to their ancient home." A prime example of this targeted branding was naming the ship that carried Jewish immigrants to Palestine in 1947 as *Exodus*. Leon Uris's best-selling novel of 1958, *Exodus*, told the story of those immigrants. The book was then made into a Hollywood

---

[12]Noura Erakat, "Whiteness as Property in Israel: Revival, Rehabilitation, and Removal," *Harvard Journal of Ethnic and Racial Justice* 31 (2015), 78–83.

[13]Arthur Allen Cohen, *The Myth of the Judeo-Christian Tradition, and Other Dissenting Essays* (New York: Schocken Books, 1971).

[14]K. Healan Gaston, *Imagining Judeo-Christian America: Religion, Secularism, and the Redefinition of Democracy,* quoted in James Loeffler, "The Problem with the 'Judeo-Christian Tradition,'" *The Atlantic*, August 1, 2020.

movie in 1960. The film was undeniably Zionist propaganda, and it had an enormous influence on how Americans and Europeans started to perceive, or better, misperceive the situation in Palestine.

Yet, for a settler colonial project to succeed, it needed continuous political support and military supplies from the "motherland." This was provided first by France and, starting in the early 1960s, by the United States. The new geostrategic, political, military, and economic alliance between the two countries was coined as a "special relationship" based on "common values."

Third Stage: Expanding the Boundaries

The outcome of the 1967 war was a turning point in the Israeli settler colonial project. Within six days, Israel was able to occupy the West Bank, the Gaza Strip, the Sinai, and the Golan Heights. While Israel was able to conquer the geography with ease, this time it could not rid itself of the demographic element. The Palestinians had learned their lesson from 1948, and a majority remained steadfast in their homes. This presented, and still presents, a major challenge to the settler colonial project's aims to control both geography and demography.

The religious connotations of the conflict were many. The name Israel chose for the war, "Six-Day," had biblical connotations by comparing the war with the six days of creation before the day of rest. The victory was branded by many as little "David"—meaning the State of Israel—defeating the monster "Goliath"—meaning the Arab world. Moreover, the conquest of East Jerusalem became the theme of the Israeli song "Jerusalem, City of Gold," which was the hit of 1967 and perpetuated the image of two thousand years of longing for the city. The song portrays the myth of Israel returning to a barren land, to dry fountains, and to the "Temple mountain." The picture of Israeli soldiers standing by the Western Wall became the iconic "religious" image of the war. Features of settler colonialism are present in these images. For then-Israeli defense minister, Moshe Dayan, this was nothing less than the reenactment of the Joshua conquest.

The victory boosted Jewish religious nationalism and triggered a settler colonial movement in the West Bank, termed ancient "Judea and Samaria," a title that was not so much a geographic description as it was a religious designation to the settler colonial claim. A process of "Judaization" of the newly conquered territories soon started. Settlers began to build Jewish settlements on every attainable hill, especially those with a biblical connection. A new leadership model emerged in Israel, the "rabbi-politician" replacing the more secular politician.[15] An attitude of triumphalism spread into all sectors of Israeli society. The appetite of Jewish archeologists after 1967 was such that many of them started to promote the idea of a greater Israel in line with the "Kingdom of David." In this post-1967 discourse, and consistent with settler colonial discourse, native Palestinian populations were seen as the Canaanites whose land had to be occupied by Israel. Also consistent with settler colonial discourse, Jewish settler groups even called openly for the ethnic cleansing of the Palestinian people, arguing on the basis of biblical passages that propagated the extermination of the Canaanites and other native groups of ancient Palestine.[16] This shift from secular to religious Judaism mirrored the political shift by Israel from alliance mainly with France to reliance on the United States. Subsequently, in 1977, there was a change in the Israeli government when the more religious and right-wing Likud party replaced the Labor party, the secular Zionist party.

---

[15]Avi Sagi and Dov Schwartz, *Religious Zionism and the Six Day War: From Realism to Messianism* (London: Routledge, 2018).

[16]Ilan Pappe, *The Ethnic Cleansing of Palestine*, 2nd ed. (London: Oneworld Publications, 2007).

The 1967 war also triggered post-Holocaust theology, a blend of liberal Christian Zionism that attempted "to revive liberal Protestant support for the Jewish State."[17] They supported the settler colonial project by propagating the "territorial dimension of Judaism."[18] This genre of Christian theology rendered the native people of the land, the Palestinians, utterly invisible, theologically erased as if the land were unpopulated: *terra nullius.* Once a unity between God, people, and land is constituted for the settler colonies, the native people are seen as aliens who do not belong to their indigenous land.

Palestinian intellectuals addressed the nature of Israel as a settler colonial project at an early stage. Organizations like the Palestine Research Center and the Institute for Palestine Studies were actively researching and publishing issues highlighting the racist and colonial nature of the Israeli state, not only against the Palestinian population but also against Arab and Black Jews. Fayez Sayegh, the director of the Palestine Research Center, published a booklet in 1965 with the title *Zionist Colonialism in Palestine* that listed several features of the "Zionist settler-state."[19] Addressing the UN General Assembly in 1975, Sayegh alluded to an important feature of the Israel settler colonial state that he coined as "pumping-in" Jewish migrants while "pumping-out" the native Palestinians.[20] Backed by support from the Soviet Union as well as African, Arab, and Muslim countries, Sayegh's words led the General Assembly of the United Nations to adopt Resolution 3379, determining "Zionism as a form of racism and

---

[17]Stephen R. Haynes, "Christian Holocaust Theology: A Critical Reassessment," *Journal of the American Academy of Religion* 62, no. 2 (1994): 562.

[18]W. D. Davies, *The Territorial Dimension of Judaism* (Berkeley: University of California Press, 1982).

[19]Fayez Abdullah Sayegh, *Zionist Colonialism in Palestine* (Beirut: Research Center, Palestine Liberation Organization, 1965).

[20]Fayez A. Sayegh, *Zionism: A Form of Racism and Racial Discrimination: Four Statements Made at the U.N. General Assembly* (New York: Office of the Permanent Observer of the Palestine Liberation Organization to the United Nations, 1976), 8.

racial discrimination."[21] Living in the United States through the 1967 War and at the height of the civil rights movement, Palestinian intellectual Edward Said—a Protestant Palestinian Christian like Sayegh—detected a form of racism against everything that was Arab or Muslim in the American media. His 1968 essay, "The Arab Portrayed," became the blueprint for Said's 1978 publication, *Orientalism*. A year later, he published "Zionism from the Standpoint of Its Victims."[22] The racism against Arabs and blind support for the Israeli occupation of the West Bank and Gaza Strip in the American media were identified by Said as mutually reliant narratives.

Fourth Stage: Negotiating a Compromise

In December 1987 the first Intifada or Palestinian uprising broke out. The pictures of Israeli tanks on one side and Palestinian kids on the other were screened on televisions worldwide, making Palestinians and their oppression under an Israeli military occupation plainly visible. It was difficult to ignore the Palestinian tragedy. Just two years later, the world watched the images of the Berlin Wall coming down as a symbol of a slowly dismantled Soviet Union. One of the last acts of the Soviet Union was to cosponsor, with the United States, the Madrid Conference in autumn 1991. With the end of the Cold War, the United States became the dominant global power, exercising tremendous influence over Israel.

Under the Bush administration, Secretary of State James Baker introduced the "land for peace" formula by which Israel would give up the 1967 occupied territories in exchange for a peace

---

[21]A/RES/3379 (XXX), November 10, 1975, https://web.archive.org/web/20121206052903/http://unispal.un.org/UNISPAL.NSF/0/761C1063530766A7052566A2005B74D1.

[22]Edward W. Said, "Zionism from the Standpoint of Its Victims," *Social Text* 1 (1979): 7–58.

treaty with the Palestinians and neighboring Arab countries. With this aim in mind, the Bush administration conditioned the soft loans given to Israel, stating that the funds were not to be used for settlement expansion. According to this rationale, peace could be achieved through political compromise that required an end to the expansion of the Jewish settler colonial project. The Madrid Conference paved the way for secret negotiations between the Palestine Liberation Organization (PLO) and the Israeli government. PLO Chairman Yasser Arafat and Israeli Foreign Minister Shimon Peres signed the Oslo Accords on the lawn of the White House on September 9, 1993.

As part of the accords, the PLO recognized the State of Israel in exchange for Israel recognizing the PLO as the representative of the Palestinian people. For the PLO, weakened and isolated as a result of the collapse of the Soviet Union and the US invasion of Iraq, the accords were a rescue rope that allowed the leadership to resettle in the West Bank and Gaza. However, just as the African National Congress in South Africa negotiated with the de Klerk government to end Apartheid and give Black South Africans their political rights without dismantling the structure of the settler colonial project, leaving the majority of Black South Africans to continue to live in Bantustans without access to economic power, the Oslo Accords gave the PLO the right to interim Palestinian self-rule in limited areas of the West Bank and the Gaza Strip, with the hope of a permanent solution within five years, without changing the structure of the Jewish settler colonial project. Postponing issues related to Jerusalem, settlements, borders, water, and refugees indicated that Israel was not ready or able to end its settler colonial project.

For Native Americans in the United States, treaties were violated and often used to buy time to further the settler colonial project. This was the case in Palestine, where the State of Israel used the pretext of negotiations to preempt the outcome, enhancing its settler colonial project in the West Bank, including

East Jerusalem. There were 110,000 Jewish settlers in 1993, and that number has now grown to over 800,000. East Jerusalem has been Judaized, the resources of the West Bank are exploited for the settler community, and no refugees have been allowed to return. Throughout this stage, Israel has continued to act as a de facto settler colonial state with the Palestinian government nothing more than a subcontractor for this state.

The Oslo Accords triggered a plethora of Palestinian Christian writing in which the spirit of the era was focused on justice, peace, or reconciliation. Other responses came from postcolonial biblical scholars, most of them living, like the Palestinians, on the margin. Robert Allen Warrior, himself a Native American, read the biblical story through the eyes of the Canaanites.[23] Born in Hong Kong, theologian Kwok Pui-Lan struggled with the question "Can I believe in a God who killed the Canaanites and who seems not to have listened to the cry of the Palestinians now for some forty years?"[24] In 1997, Michael Prior clearly demonstrated "how the biblical account has been used to justify the conquest of land in different regions and at different periods, focusing on the Spanish and Portuguese colonization and settlement of Latin America, the white settlement in southern Africa, and the Zionist conquest and settlement in Palestine."[25]

Jewish theological voices also started to be heard critiquing the policies of the State of Israel. Marc Ellis was, perhaps, the most vocal among them.[26] The focus of theological writings

---

[23]Robert Allen Warrior, "A North American Perspective: Canaanites, Cowboys, and Indians," in *Voices from the Margin: Interpreting the Bible in the Third World*, 25th anniv. ed., ed. R. S. Sugirtharajah (Maryknoll, NY: Orbis Books, 2016), 235–41.

[24]Pui-lan Kwok, *Discovering the Bible in the Non-Biblical World* (Eugene, OR: Wipf and Stock, 2003), 99.

[25]Michael Prior, *The Bible and Colonialism: A Moral Critique* (Sheffield, UK: Continuum International, 1997), 11.

[26]Marc H. Ellis, *Israel and Palestine—Out of the Ashes: The Search For Jewish Identity in the Twenty-First Century* (London: Pluto Press, 2002); Marc H. Ellis,

during the earlier years of this era was on Israeli occupation as something temporary rather than a structure of settler colonialism. However, in recent years, several scholars like Nur Masalha, Fernando Segovia, Mitri Raheb, Santiago Slabodsky, and others have begun to write about the land issue using a decolonial, postcolonial, or cultural-critical approach.[27] Steven Salaita has furthered this work in his groundbreaking comparative analysis of Native American and Palestinian literature, showing how settler colonial societies weaponize biblical stories as national histories to justify their colonial projects.[28]

Fifth Stage: Sealing the Settler Colonial Project

In recent years, we have witnessed a certain pattern repeating itself in Israeli politics. This pattern has occurred within a context of change shaped by the election of President Trump in the United States, the rise of populism and Christian Zion-

Toward a Jewish Theology of Liberation: Foreword by Desmond Tutu and Gustavo Gutierrez, 3rd ed. (Waco, TX: Baylor University Press, 2011).

[27]Nur Masalha, *Expulsion of the Palestinians: The Concept of "Transfer" in Zionist Political Thought, 1882–1948* (Washington, DC: Institute for Palestine Studies, 1992); Nur Masalha, *Imperial Israel and the Palestinians: The Politics of Expansion* (Sterling, VA: Pluto Press, 2000); Nur Masalha, *The Politics of Denial: Israel and the Palestinian Refugee Problem* (London: Pluto Press, 2003); Nur Masalha, *The Bible and Zionism: Invented Traditions, Archaeology and Post-Colonialism in Palestine-Israel* (London: Zed Books, 2007); Nur Masalha, *The Palestine Nakba: Decolonising History, Narrating the Subaltern, Reclaiming Memory* (New York: Zed Books, 2012); Nur Masalha, *The Zionist Bible: Biblical Precedent, Colonialism and the Erasure of Memory* (London: Routledge, 2014); Fernando F. Segovia, "Engaging the Palestinian Theological-Critical Project of Liberation: A Critical Dialogue," in *The Biblical Text in the Context of Occupation: Towards a New Hermeneutics of Liberation*, ed. Mitri Raheb (Bethlehem: CreateSpace Independent Publishing Platform, 2012), 29–80; Mitri Raheb, *Faith in the Face of Empire: The Bible through Palestinian Eyes* (Maryknoll, NY: Orbis Books, 2014); S. Slabodsky, *Decolonial Judaism: Triumphal Failures of Barbaric Thinking* (New York: Palgrave Macmillan, 2014).

[28]Salaita, *Holy Land in Transit*; Salaita, *Inter/Nationalism*.

ism worldwide, the reelection of Netanyahu, the weakening of Arab countries, the dividing of Palestinian territory with political divisions (West Bank versus Gaza), and the increase of an Israel-friendlier Gulf region.[29] The first significant move in this era was made by President Trump in December 2017, when he recognized Jerusalem as Israel's capital, followed by the opening of the US Embassy in the city six months later.[30] In July 2018, the Israel Knesset passed the so-called Nation-State Bill that defined Israel as the nation-state of the Jewish people.[31] The next move came from President Trump in March 2019, when he recognized Israeli sovereignty over the occupied Golan Heights.[32] In all of these moves, the pattern has been to legalize what is not legal, thus transforming a de facto status into a de jure one. East Jerusalem, the West Bank, and the Golan Heights are occupied territories according to international law although they are effectively under Israeli control.[33] Palestinians inside Israel, for example, comprise over 20 percent of the population and have been de facto second-class citizens; the new Nation-State Law made them legally second-class citizens.

While these moves were motivated by real political calculations by a president in need of Jewish votes and support from

[29]Mitri Raheb, "Jerusalem in the Age of Trump," in *Jerusalem: Religious, National and International Dimensions*, ed. Mitri Raheb (Bethlehem: Diyar, 2019), 23–34.

[30]"President Donald J. Trump's Proclamation on Jerusalem as the Capital of the State of Israel" https://trumpwhitehouse.archives.gov/briefings-statements/president-donald-j-trumps-proclamation-jerusalem-capital-state-israel/, December 6, 2017.

[31]Raoul Wootliff, "Final Text of Jewish Nation-State Law, Approved by the Knesset Early on July 19," *Times of Israel*, July 18, 2018, https://www.timesofisrael.com/final-text-of-jewish-nation-state-bill-set-to-become-law/.

[32]"Proclamation on Recognizing the Golan Heights as Part of the State of Israel," https://trumpwhitehouse.archives.gov/presidential-actions/proclamation-recognizing-golan-heights-part-state-israel/, March 25, 2019.

[33]B'Tselem, "The Occupied Territories and International Law," November 11, 2017, https://www.btselem.org/international_law.

his evangelical base, President Trump was aware that settler colonialism is deeply entrenched in American culture, especially through the ideology of Manifest Destiny. When the United States looks in the mirror, it does not see itself, but rather, Israel. And when it looks at Israel, it sees itself: both are settler nations who occupied the lands of native peoples and pushed those people into small reservations. In his speech at the Israel Knesset, Vice President Pence affirmed the bond between the two:

> During his historic visit to Jerusalem, President Trump declared that the bond between us, in his words, is "woven together in the hearts of our people," and the people of the United States have always held a special affection and admiration for the people of the Book. In the story of the Jews, we've always seen the story of America. It is the story of an exodus, a journey from persecution to freedom, a story that shows the power of faith and the promise of hope. My country's very first settlers also saw themselves as pilgrims, sent by Providence, to build a new Promised Land. The songs and stories of the people of Israel were their anthems, and they faithfully taught them to their children, and do to this day . . . And down through the generations, the American people became fierce advocates of the Jewish people's aspiration to return to the land of your forefathers, to claim your own new birth of freedom in your beloved homeland.[34]

In all of this, the role of the Christian Zionist and the Jewish Zionist must not be underestimated. The influence of Zionists was patently obvious at the opening of the US Embassy in

---

[34]"Full Transcript of Pence's Knesset Speech—The Jerusalem Post," January 23, 2018, https://www.jpost.com/Israel-News/Full-transcript-of-Pences-Knesset-speech-539476.

Jerusalem. It is no accident that those present at the opening ceremony were either Christian Zionists, like the two evangelical pastors John Hagee and Robert Jeffress; right-wing Israeli politicians such as Netanyahu and his political allies; or Jewish-Americans who support Israeli colonization of the West Bank, like Trump's son-in-law Jared Kushner, the American Ambassador to Israel David Friedman, Trump's special envoy Jason Greenblatt, and the casino mogul Sheldon Adelson.

Two Christian Zionist pastors were given an active role in the opening of the US Embassy in Jerusalem and delivered two prayers. Robert Jeffress, pastor of the First Baptist Church in Dallas and a televangelist, opened his prayer by saying,

> Heavenly Father, we come before you, the God of Abraham, Isaac, and Jacob, thanking you for bringing us to this momentous occasion in the life of your people and in the history of our world. Four thousand years ago, you said to your servant Abraham that you would make him the father of a great nation, a nation through whom the whole world would be blessed, and now as we look back, we see how Israel has been that blessing to the entire world.[35]

What is remarkable about this prayer is its selectivity. It highlights the genealogical line from Abraham to Jacob, through Isaac, to the State of Israel of the twenty-first century. In other words, for Jeffress, the Jews of Israel today are the direct descendants of the Patriarchs. In the pastor's view, Abraham is not only the Patriarch of the Hebrew Bible and the father of a great nation, but this nation is clearly modern Israel. Vice President Pence was one of the main advocates of the embassy relocation. The former vice president, a baptized Catholic, considers himself

---

[35]"Dr. Robert Jeffress: Opening Prayer at the U.S. Embassy Dedication in Jerusalem," May 14, 2018, https://www.youtube.com/watch?v=jSGSSisCT7E.

a born-again evangelical Christian and belongs to a movement known as Christian Zionism.[36] Pence referred to the Bible, and specifically to King David, to explain the move of the US Embassy. In his speech at the Israeli Knesset, he said,

> The Jewish people's unbreakable bond to this sacred city reaches back more than 3,000 years. It was here in Jerusalem, on Mount Moriah, that Abraham offered his son Isaac, and was credited with righteousness for his faith in God. It was here in Jerusalem, that King David consecrated the capital of the Kingdom of Israel. And since its rebirth, the modern State of Israel has called this city the seat of its government. Jerusalem is Israel's capital.[37]

In this passage of his speech, Pence reiterates Israeli propaganda that Jerusalem was consecrated the capital of "Israel" by King David three thousand years ago and should, therefore, be the "eternal capital" of the State of Israel today. Again, Pence's speech demonstrates how biblical stories are seen as a history directly connected to the present day. King David was evoked to give the transfer of the US Embassy to Jerusalem a biblical foundation in the full knowledge that the move was a violation of international law. For these Christian Zionists, when the message of the Bible as they understand it collides with international law, the Bible or divine rights take precedence over human rights. It should be no wonder that John Hagee, at the embassy opening,

---

[36]Goran Gunner and Robert O. Smith, eds., *Comprehending Christian Zionism: Perspectives in Comparison* (Minneapolis: Fortress Press, 2014); M. Raheb, "Palestinian Christian Reflections on Christian Zionism," in *Comprehending Christian Zionism: Perspectives in Comparison*, ed. Goran Gunner and Robert Smith (Minneapolis: Fortress Press, 2014); Stephen Sizer, *Zion's Christian Soldiers? The Bible, Israel and the Church*, (Nottingham, UK: Intervarsity Press, 2007); Donald E. Wagner, *Anxious for Armageddon: A Call to Partnership for Middle Eastern and Western Christians*, (Scottsdale, AZ: Herald Press, 1995).

[37]"Full Transcript of Pence's Knesset Speech."

referred to the United Nations as the axis of evil. In his prayer, he continued,

> Shout it from the housetops that Israel lives; let every Islamic terrorist hear this message, Israel lives; let it be heard in the halls of the United Nations, Israel lives; let it echo down the marble halls of the presidential palace in Iran, Israel lives; let it be known to all men that Israel lives; because he that keepeth Israel neither slumbers nor sleeps.[38]

The United Nations, with its international laws, treaties, and conventions, has now become part of the axis of evil. This fits well with Christian Zionist rhetoric and its stance toward international agency. For Hagee and Christian Zionism, God stands clearly and unapologetically on the side of Israel (and its settler colonial influence, the United States) and against international law.

The Peace for Prosperity Conference, held by the Trump administration in Bahrain on June 26, 2019, continued the clear connection of US Zionist biblical interpretation and Israeli settler colonial activity.[39] The name chosen for the conference implies that the prosperity of Palestinians is America's intention if Palestinians would only walk with the Trump administration, alluding to the so-called prosperity gospel. Just as the prosperity gospel was used to exploit the poor, so this conference attempted to exploit Palestinian rights and resources. While Jared Kushner was introducing his fifty-billion-dollar plan "in support of the Palestinians," his colleague Jason Greenblatt was cutting all funding to UNRWA (United Nations Relief and

---

[38]Pastor John Hagee Historic Prayer at Opening of US Embassy in Jerusalem, Israel, 2018, https://www.youtube.com/watch?v=ll6n4ELuoMQ.

[39]"Peace to Prosperity," https://trumpwhitehouse.archives.gov/peacetoprosperity/economic/empowering-palestinian-people/, accessed April 24, 2023.

Works Agency) for Palestinian refugees.[40] While Kushner spoke about transforming the health care system in the West Bank and Gaza, Greenblatt cut all American funding to Palestinian hospitals in Jerusalem.

The plan was deceptive, talking about 50 billion dollars in support of Palestine while half of the amount will actually go to neighboring countries: Egypt, Jordan, Lebanon, and, significantly, Israel. Since the funds would be managed by international corporations, another 20 percent would be deducted as management fees. All told, less than 20 billion dollars would be invested over 10 years, an amount that is less than the actual cost of the Israeli occupation, estimated at 6.9 billion dollars per year.[41] The funds to neighboring countries aim to upgrade their ports and airports, while Palestinians are not even given a promise of their own port or airport. The plan promises to double the potable water supply to Palestinians at a time when Israel confiscates 82 percent of the West Bank water resources, meaning that at least two-thirds of water aquifers in the West Bank would remain under Israeli control.[42] The plan promises to construct a new power plant in Gaza so that, within ten years, the population in Gaza would have sixteen hours of daily electricity. Yet, who can guarantee that Israel will not destroy this power plant like the one they destroyed in 2014?[43] That power plant was paid for by private American and Palestinian

---

[40]"US Ends Aid to Palestinian Refugee Agency UNRWA," *BBC News*, September 1, 2018, sec. US & Canada, https://www.bbc.com/news/world-us-canada-45377336.

[41]"The Real Cost of Israel's Occupation of the Palestinians," *Haaretz.com*, November 16, 2011, https://www.haaretz.com/1.5210115.

[42]"The Occupation of Water," November 29, 2017, https://www.amnesty.org/en/latest/campaigns/2017/11/the-occupation-of-water/.

[43]Harriet Sherwood, "Gaza's Only Power Plant Destroyed in Israel's Most Intense Air Strike Yet," *The Guardian*, July 30, 2014, sec. World News, https://www.theguardian.com/world/2014/jul/29/gaza-power-plant-destroyed-israeli-airstrike-100-palestinians-dead.

investors and had been supplying Gaza with electricity twenty-four hours per day, every day.

Kushner's plan promised to leverage investment into the Palestinian tourism industry. Yet, the most important hub for the Palestinian tourism industry is East Jerusalem. If Jerusalem is off the table, what remains are the crumbs. Furthermore, if Jewish settlers continue to occupy important archeological sites like Qumran, Herodium, and the Dead Sea, then even less remains for the Palestinians. The plan promises to "upgrade border crossings" (a euphemism for checkpoints), to "reduce trade barriers," and to "reduce the complications of transport and travel." Barriers and checkpoints would not be removed, only upgraded. Palestinians would still be living under the thumb of Israeli soldiers who control their movements. The promise to build "special access roads at major crossing points" would further entrench the two-road system in the West Bank, one for Jewish Israeli colonizers and the other for the native Palestinians, and enshrine the already-existing apartheid system.[44]

The map attached to the plan shows that Israel would annex the most fertile Palestinian land, including the Jordan Valley and the western slopes of the Jerusalem–Hebron mountains, which constitute the food basket for the West Bank. The map shows that Palestinian cities would become permanent enclaves or Bantustans with no territorial continuity, connected only via underground tunnels or bridges.[45] While the plan promises prosperity, it does exactly the opposite: exploitation.

In a different connection to scripture, the plan reminds me of the story of the temptation of Jesus. In the gospel account, the devil took Jesus "to a very high mountain and showed him all

[44]See B'Tselem, "Apartheid," https://www.btselem.org/topic/apartheid.

[45]State of Palestine, Palestine Liberation Organization, Negotiations Affairs Department, "Looming Annexation: Israel's Denial of Palestine's Right to Exist," June 30, 2020, https://www.nad.ps/sites/default/files/06302020.pdf.

the kingdoms of the world and their splendor. 'All this I will give you,' he said, 'if you will bow down and worship me'" (Matthew 4:8–9). The plan promises prosperity for the Palestinians while denying them justice, colonizing their land, exploiting their natural resources, and robbing them of dignity and freedom.

On September 15, 2020, Trump signed the so-called Abraham Accords with the foreign ministers of the United Arab Emirates and Bahrain, and the Israeli prime minister. Biblical language was utilized here as well. The Accords started by recognizing

> that the Arab and Jewish peoples are descendants of a common ancestor, Abraham, and inspired, in that spirit, to foster in the Middle East a reality in which Muslims, Jews, Christians and peoples of all faiths, denominations, beliefs and nationalities live in, and are committed to, a spirit of coexistence, mutual understanding and mutual respect.[46]

This same metaphor was used by Vice President Pence in his address to the Knesset on January 22, 2018.

> The winds of change can already be witnessed across the Middle East. Longstanding enemies are becoming partners. Old foes are finding new grounds for cooperation. And the descendants of Isaac and Ishmael are coming together in common cause as never before. Last year in Saudi Arabia, President Trump addressed an unprecedented gathering of leaders from more than fifty nations at the Arab-Islamic American Summit. He challenged the people of this region

---

[46]"Abraham Accord Peace Agreement: Treaty of Peace, Diplomatic Relations and Full Normalization between the United Arab Emirates and the State of Israel," September 15, 2020, https://www.state.gov/wp-content/uploads/2020/09/UAE_Israel-treaty-signed-FINAL-15-Sept-2020-508.pdf.

to work ever closer together, to recognize shared opportunities, and to confront shared challenges.[47]

Pence reiterated in his speech a common belief that Arabs and Muslims are the descendants of Ishmael. Ishmael is Abraham's son, yet he is still the son of a slave and the one excluded from the promise. In this biblical language, Ishmael remains inferior to Isaac. Isaac's supremacy over Ishmael is taken at face value and has been used repeatedly by White supremacists to subjugate Black people, African Americans, First Nations, Arabs, Muslims, and the Palestinians.

Analysis of the Abraham Accords clearly shows that the goal had little to do with securing peace among the parties of the accord. Israel was never even at war with Bahrain, the United Arab Emirates, or Morocco. Unofficial relations between Israel and Bahrain, the United Arab Emirates, and Morocco go back to the early 1970s.

The Abraham Accords had a different function: to leverage Israel as a broker with the Trump administration so that Arab monarchs could obtain what they wanted from the United States but were unable to get directly. For Israel, the accord with the United Arab Emirates meant tightening the ring on Iran, getting closer to its borders, and, thereby, threatening it. At the same time, the accords were intended to isolate and bypass the Palestinian people by normalizing Israeli relations with some Arab countries. The Trump–Netanyahu "deal" within the accords was to grant the request of each Arab state ready to sign a peace agreement with Israel.

The Abraham Accords were widely celebrated as a breakthrough and the beginning of a new chapter in Israeli-Arab relations. Yet, the Abraham Accords must be seen within the larger Middle Eastern geopolitical context. Via the accords,

---

[47]"Full Transcript of Pence's Knesset Speech."

Israel was able to draw closer to three vibrant waterways of the region: the Strait of Hormuz, the Strait of Gibraltar, and the Strait of Tiran. With Trump planning to repatriate American troops from the Middle East, Israel was selected to continue US policing by proxy, securing oil transportation routes.

The culmination of the Trump policy was the so-called "Deal of the Century," which envisioned the annexation of the rest of Palestinian prime land and resources in the West Bank. The annexation plan aimed to change the status of the West Bank from occupied territory to being under full Israeli sovereignty. With the backing of President Trump and his team of Jewish American settler supporters (particularly Friedman, the American Ambassador to Israel, and Greenblatt, Trump's special envoy), Israel felt that the time had come to fulfill a long-standing dream of Greater Israel, thus sealing the settler colonial project. For several reasons, Israel decided not to proceed legally with its annexation plan of the West Bank, but rather to continue with a silent and de facto annexation. This decision has created a de facto system of apartheid on both sides of the Green Line. Although the Biden administration continues to express opposition to the Jewish settlement project, Israel is currently allowed to proceed with settlement and is provided political impunity by its settler colonialist ally, the United States.

2

Christian Zionism

The Christian Lobby
Supporting Settler Colonization in Palestine

In the late 1980s, I was invited to lecture to a group of German theology students studying at the Hebrew University in Jerusalem. The program, *Studium in Israel,* aims to bring Protestant theology students to Israel for a year to study Judaism on the path to creating the next generation of pastors and theologians committed to Jewish–Christian dialogue. A well-known German professor of systematic theology named Friedrich Wilhelm Marquardt also attended the lecture. Following my presentation, we engaged the students in a dialogue with a focus on Christian theology in the Palestinian context. Professor Marquardt intervened and declared in front of all the students, "Mr. Raheb, you stand in God's way." Marquardt continued, "If I were you, I would pack my bag and emigrate, leaving this country to its rightful owners, the Jews." I was shocked and speechless. I was still a very young pastor, not even thirty, and I wondered how this German professor dared to question my belonging to the land of my forebears? What hubris was it to ask me to leave my homeland and make way for Jewish settlers? What kind of a theology is this?

Marquardt was not an evangelical or fundamentalist Christian obsessed with prophecy or eschatology like those I mentioned in the previous chapter. He was a sophisticated German theologian who grew up among the practice of critical-historical methodology. Marquardt was by no means a right-wing Christian. On the contrary, he was a socialist Christian, but he was someone we can still describe as a Christian Zionist. In fact, many of the German students who graduate from this program in Jerusalem end up becoming what we might call Christian Zionists.

Marquardt and his students do not fit the traditional description of Christian Zionism. Most of the writings on Christian Zionism focus almost exclusively on Christian dispensationalists who are obsessed with Old Testament prophecies and End Times scenarios. This description may be the traditional case because many of the publications about Christian Zionism were written by evangelical theologians attempting to show that Christian Zionist interpretation is not compatible with sound biblical teaching, as if an agreed standard teaching even exists. These publications represent a form of intra-evangelical dialogue on biblical hermeneutics that pays little attention to the phenomenon of Christian Zionism. Furthermore, when mainline scholars write about Christian Zionism, they usually dismiss its followers as fundamentalists, literalists, and fanatics. They do not examine the phenomenon in its entirety. To reduce followers of Christian Zionism to dispensationalists or literalists does not do justice to the phenomenon of Christian Zionism. This narrow focus ignores another important group: that of the liberal, scholarly, and subtle Christian Zionists, the Christian Zionism of Marquardt and his students, which is every bit as dangerous as that of Christian dispensationalists. More importantly, this narrow focus does not enable us to grasp the breadth and depth of this dangerous phenomenon.

Christian Zionism: Redefined

The phenomenon of Christian Zionism comes in many shapes and manifestations. It is deeply rooted in evangelical circles, and it is present in mainline churches as well as in liberal theology. It had its roots in Europe, branched out to North America, and is today widespread in the Global South. For this reason, there is a dire need today for a new approach to and definition of Christian Zionism that encompasses the wide range of its manifestations. Therefore, I argue that Christian Zionism should be defined as a Christian lobby that supports the Jewish settler colonialism of Palestinian land by using biblical/theological constructs within a metanarrative while taking glocal considerations into account. This definition is less focused on the biblical discourse of Christian Zionists, which can vary considerably from literalists to post-Holocaust theologians, from very conservative to liberal. In fact, the biblical/theological rationale espoused by the majority of Christian Zionists is vague and based on a few varied verses from the Bible. The emphasis of my proposed definition is on the lobbying aspect of Christian Zionism: not on what people *believe* but what they *do* based on that belief. It is naïve to think that a few biblical passages power Christian Zionism.

The Christian Zionist narrative is always embedded within a metanarrative so that those who espouse it do not see themselves as engaged in pure political lobbying, but rather as agents of a grand plan from which they read and interpret both scripture and history. Alongside the metanarrative, Christian Zionists are always connected to "glocal" issues and considerations, thereby combining their ideas with struggles and fears in specific contexts. This combination is what makes Christian Zionism so dangerous. While they lobby for "Israel," they are actually lobbying for other issues that are important to their specific context. Finally, Christian Zionist support for the Jewish colonial settler has less to do with "head knowledge" than with "heart knowledge."[1] As such, it cannot be fought by a biblical or theological counterargument from rational reasoning. The metanarrative changes, depending on time and place, and glocal considerations vary depending on the context. Christian Zionists have in common an emotional attachment to the Zionist settler colonial project in Palestine. In this approach, the hermeneutical key to understanding Christian Zionism is not so much the biblical or theological interpretive moves, but rather the lobbying action in support of a settler colonialist movement. In this chapter, I will apply this new definition of Christian Zionism to three different manifestations of Christian Zionism within three different contexts that have had major implications on the situation in Palestine.

Christian Zionism and the British Empire

The Anglo-Saxon world was obsessed with Jews and Judaism from the time of the Reformation. Judeo-centric prophecy interpretation developed over several centuries to become an important theme in British intellectual discourse.[2] However, what was a theological construct started to become *realpolitik* in the age of the British Empire thanks to three prominent Christian Zionists within the British establishment: Shaftesbury, Churchill, and Balfour.

Anthony Ashley Cooper, known as the Seventh Earl of

---

[1]As an example, see Aron Engberg, " 'A Fool for Christ:' Sense-Making and Negotiation of Identity in the Life Story of a Christian Soldier," in *Comprehending Christian Zionism: Perspectives in Comparison*, ed. Goran Gunner and Robert O. Smith (Minneapolis: Fortress Press, 2014), 33–59.

[2]Robert O. Smith, *More Desired Than Our Own Salvation: The Roots of Christian Zionism* (New York: Oxford University Press, 2013), 114.

Shaftesbury, was a prominent figure in the evangelical Anglican movement and a member of the British House of Commons.[3] Shaftesbury followed developments in Palestine in the 1830s very closely. Following the occupation of Palestine by Ibrahim Pasha in 1831, Shaftesbury became active in establishing a British presence there. He was instrumental in opening the British consulate in Jerusalem in 1838 as well as in establishing the Bishopric of the United Church of England and Ireland in 1841. In January 1839 and just a few weeks after the opening of the consulate, Shaftesbury published an article in the *Quarterly Review* calling for the settlement of British Jews in Palestine.

> The soil and climate of Palestine are singularly adapted to the growth of produce required for the exigencies of Great Britain; the finest cotton may be obtained in almost unlimited abundance; silk and madder are the staple of the country, and olive oil is now, as it ever was, the very fatness of the land. Capital and skill are alone required: the presence of a British officer, and the increased security of property which his presence will confer, may invite them from these islands to the cultivation of Palestine; and the Jews, who will betake themselves to agriculture in no other land, having found, in the English consul, a mediator between their people and the Pacha, will probably return in yet greater numbers, and become once more the husbandmen of Judaea and Galilee.[4]

The second person who was instrumental in supporting the settler colonial project in Palestine was Charles Henry Churchill, the British consul in Ottoman Syria. Less than four

---

[3]For more on Lord Shaftesbury, see Donald M. Lewis, *The Origins of Christian Zionism: Lord Shaftesbury and Evangelical Support for a Jewish Homeland*, reprint ed. (Cambridge: Cambridge University Press, 2014).

[4]Shaftesbury, as quoted in Nur Masalha, *The Zionist Bible: Biblical Precedent, Colonialism and the Erasure of Memory* (London: Routledge, 2014), 83.

months after the defeat of Ibrahim Pasha's troops in Palestine (on June 14, 1841), Churchill wrote a letter to Sir Moses Montefiore, the president of the Board of Deputies of British Jews, proposing a strategy for Jewish settlement in Palestine. In this letter, we read,

> I cannot conceal from you my most anxious desire to see your countrymen endeavour once more to resume their existence as a people . . .Were the resources which you all possess steadily directed towards the regeneration of Syria and Palestine, there cannot be a doubt but that, under the blessing of the Most High, those countries would amply repay the undertaking, and that you would end by obtaining the sovereignty of at least Palestine. Syria and Palestine, in a word, must be taken under European protection and governed in the sense and according to the spirit of European administration.[5]

Unsure of how his intentions might be interpreted, Churchill was keen to clarify his motives to a British Jewish banker and philanthropist like Montefiore. He continued,

> If you think otherwise, I shall bend at once to your decision, only begging you to appreciate my motive, which is simply an ardent desire for the welfare and prosperity of a people to whom we all owe our possession of those blessed truths which direct our minds with unerring faith to the enjoyment of another and better world.[6]

---

[5]Lucien Wolf, *Notes on the Diplomatic History of the Jewish Question: With Texts of Protocols, Treaty Stipulations and Other Public Acts and Official Documents* (London: Spottiswoode, 1919), 119, http://archive.org/details/notesondiplomati00wolfuoft.

[6]Ibid., 121.

The British colonial project in Palestine was pursued at every political opportunity. In the context of the Crimean War (1853–56), Shaftesbury expressed in his diary his idea of a settler colonial project in Palestine more bluntly:

> The Turkish Empire is in rapid decay; every nation is restless; all hearts expect some great things . . . No one can say that we are anticipating prophecy; the requirements of it [prophecy] seem nearly fulfilled; Syria "is wasted without an inhabitant"; these vast and fertile regions will soon be without a ruler, without a known and acknowledged power to claim domination. The territory must be assigned to someone or other; can it be given to any European potentate? To any American colony? To any Asiatic sovereign or tribe? Are these aspirants from Africa to fasten a demand on the soil from Hamath to the river of Egypt? No, no, no! There is a country without a nation; a nation without a country. His own once loved, nay, still loved people, the sons of Abraham, of Isaac, and of Jacob.[7]

The seeds planted by Shaftesbury and Churchill bore fruit. In 1860, Sir Moses Montefiore sponsored the establishment of the first Jewish colony in Palestine, just outside the Old City in Jerusalem. Yet, it was the outcome of WWI that gave Britain the final say over the fate of Palestine. On November 2, 1917, the First Earl of Balfour, Lord Arthur James Balfour, the British foreign secretary, wrote to his colleague in Parliament and the prominent British Jewish banker, Baron Walter Rothschild (1868–1937), announcing his government's support to establish "a national home for the Jewish people" in Palestine.

---

[7]Edwin Hodder, *The Life and Work of the Seventh Earl of Shaftesbury, K.G.* ATLA Monograph Preservation Program; ATLA Fiche 1988–1276 (London: Cassell, 1886), 14.

To facilitate the permanent settlement of European Jews in Palestine, Britain lobbied for the Mandate on Palestine, and this was granted on April 25, 1920, by the League of Nations. While all other mandates were to "prepare the natives for independence," the British Mandate over Palestine was to prepare Palestine for a Jewish settler colonial project on a land where 95 percent of the population were Arab Palestinians. In defending this decision before the House of Lords in 1922, Balfour explained the theological motives behind his colonial policy.

The policy we initiated is likely to prove a successful policy. But we have never pretended that it was purely from these materialist considerations that the declaration originally sprang . . . It is in order that we may send a message that will tell them [the Jews] that Christendom is not oblivious to their faith, that it is not unmindful of the service they have rendered to the religions of the world, and most of all to the religion that the majority of Your Lordships' house profess, and that we desire to the best of our ability to give them that opportunity of developing in peace and quietness under British rule, those great gifts which hitherto they have been compelled to bring to fruition in countries that know not their language and belong not to their race. That is the ideal which I desire to see accomplished, that is the aim which lay at the root of the policy I am trying to defend; and, though it is defensible on every ground, that is the ground that chiefly moves me.[8]

The three quotations above demonstrate the key features of Christian Zionism. All three British diplomats worked diligently to initiate and support a Jewish settler colonial project in Pales-

---

[8]Blanche E. C. Dugdale, *Arthur James Balfour, 1906–1930* (New York: Putnam's Sons, 1937), 58.

tine. All aspects of settler colonialism are obvious: Palestine is perceived as "a land without a people" to be designated by the British Empire for "a people without a land." For Shaftesbury, the land is barren, yet it has great agricultural potential to serve the colonial interests and needs of the British Empire. The native population of Palestine are mostly invisible and certainly lack political rights. The intruders are perceived, based on biblical assumptions, as natives belonging to the colonized land. The native inhabitants, Christians and Muslims who made up 95 percent of the population, were portrayed negatively by Balfour as "non-Jewish communities" who might have "civil and religious rights," but no national rights or sovereignty over their land. The land was to be settled permanently by European Jews who possessed the capital and skills needed to "develop" the land, meaning to subdue it to British imperial interests. In return, the British Empire would provide protection for the Jewish settlers.

All three politicians were devout evangelical Christians; all three based their ideas on religious beliefs that were entwined with Western imperial interests. Their biblical and theological rationale is vague and is not always expressed clearly. Yet, in the background is a feeling, and to some degree a conviction, that the modern-day Jews are somehow directly connected to the biblical Patriarchs and, thus, entitled to the land of Palestine. Only Shaftesbury seems to be motivated by biblical prophecy per se.

Shaftesbury, Churchill, and Balfour fit the definition of Christian Zionists, as they were active lobbyists for a settler colonial project in Palestinian land. The overarching metanarrative is clear in their case: their main interest was to further the interests of the British Empire with the British Jews as the subcontractors of imperial expansion. Yet, other and often unspoken glocal considerations had a significant influence on their actions. Balfour, for example, perceived Jews to be strangers who do not belong to Europe because of their language and race. Sending British Jews to Palestine would both serve British imperial interests and, in the silent hope of British politicians, solve the European Jewish question in Great Britain. British politicians were uneasy with the political and economic influence of British Jewry inside Britain and concerned by the waves of impoverished East European Jewish migrants flooding into Britain. Combined with the Aliens Act of 1905, the settler colonial project in Palestine would prevent Jews arriving to Britain from Russia by diverting them to their "homeland" of Palestine. With this work, Christian Zionists preceded Jewish Zionism by half a century and, in fact, triggered the latter movement.

Liberal Christian Zionism and the Holocaust

The British Mandate over Palestine ended on May 14, 1948. On that day, Jews, based on what they called their "natural and historic rights," in conjunction with the UN Partition Plan of 1947, declared their state with the biblical name of Israel. The declaration itself was drafted using more secular language and refrained from using any religious justification for the state. The declaration spoke of the necessity for a state for the Jews given the catastrophe that had led to the "massacre of millions of Jews in Europe." Realizing that the Holocaust would not have been possible without Christian anti-Judaism, cultural stereotyping, and political scapegoating of Jews and their religion, many Western Christians searched for new ways to relate to Judaism. One of the first theological attempts came from Holland.

In 1949, the General Synod of the Dutch Reformed Church adopted "dialogue with Israel" as the calling of the church.[9] A similar breakthrough in relations with Jews and Judaism based

---

[9]Walter Kickel, *das gelobte Land* (Munich: Kösel, 1984), 159.

on "the patrimony of Abraham" was accomplished in *Nostra Aetate*[10] adopted by the Second Vatican Council in 1965. These attempts represent a desire to combat anti-Semitism and to start a meaningful dialogue while learning from a painful history. There is no doubt that this was a noble cause that was long overdue. However, it was exactly this painful history that triggered liberal Christian Zionism, known as post-Holocaust theology, and led several mainline European churches to adopt Zionist discourse into their confessional documents.

This brand of liberal Christian Zionism was triggered by Jewish writers and theologians who struggled with the meaning of the Holocaust. In 1960, Elie Wiesel's bestseller *Night*, published in English, focused on his experiences as a Jewish Holocaust survivor in Auschwitz and Buchenwald.[11] Six years later, the Jewish theologian Richard Rubenstein published *After Auschwitz: Radical Theology and Contemporary Judaism*, questioning the possibility of faith in God after Auschwitz.[12] Emil Fackenheim stressed the uniqueness of the Holocaust compared with other modern evils such as Hiroshima, Vietnam, or the enslavement of Africans. Irving Greenberg spoke of the Holocaust and the establishment of the State of Israel as a "third era" of Jewish history, where the State of Israel could assert national self-interests based on military power without apologies or illusions.

The Jewish theological qualification of the Holocaust led churches and liberal Christian theologians to make the Holocaust the hermeneutical key for Christian theology after 1967. The 1967 war was instrumental to this effort, as the resounding

[10]James M. Barrens, *In Our Time (Nostra Aetate): How Catholics and Jews Built a New Relationship* (St. Petersburg, FL: Mr. Media Books, 2015); Kail C. Ellis, ed., *Nostra Aetate, Non-Christian Religions, and Interfaith Relations* (Cham, Switzerland: Palgrave Macmillan, 2020).

[11]Elie Wiesel, *Night*, trans. Marion Wiesel (New York: Hill and Wang, 2006).

[12]Richard L. Rubenstein, *After Auschwitz: Radical Theology and Contemporary Judaism* (Indianapolis: Bobbs-Merrill, 1966).

Israeli victory triggered Jewish messianism as well as Christian Zionism. Starting in the sixties, a Zionist political narrative of "unity of God, land, and people" and a "theological attribute to the State of Israel" became important features of Protestant liberal theologies. Karl Barth was one of the theologians to describe the State of Israel in 1962 as a new sign of God's faithfulness to the seeds of Abraham, thus giving a political entity a theological qualification.[13] Anglo-Saxon churches adopted the Zionist construct of God, land (Palestine), and people (Jewish people), thus giving the Jewish settlers the needed theological discourse to market their settler colonialism in the West. Racialization played a further role: European Jews were perceived as civilized, White, and the indigenous owners of the land, while Arabs with a Muslim majority were portrayed as non-White terrorists, another feature of settler colonialism. African Americans and Palestinians felt oppressed by the same forces, resulting in a transnational alliance for liberation between the Black Panther Party and the Palestine Liberation Organization.

While conservative millenialist Christians admired the Israeli victory in 1967, liberal Christian Zionists were perplexed. A different outcome could have resulted in the annihilation of Jews in the State of Israel, a potential new Holocaust. From then on, liberal Christian theologians started to see themselves as the defenders of Jews and lobbyists for the State of Israel. As examples, I would like to focus on two churches and two post-Holocaust theologians.

On June 16, 1970, the General Synod of the Dutch Reformed Church adopted a first-of-its-kind church statement entitled *Israel: People, Land and State*.[14] In the section on "The Jewish people in the Old Testament," the statement emphasized that "biblical Israel" was not only a religious community but also

---

[13]Kickel, *das gelobte Land*, 186.
[14]Ibid., 158–66.

a historical reality. With these words, the Dutch Reformed Church adopted the Zionist self-understanding of Jews not so much as a religious community but as a people and, thus, a nation. The document also borrowed the Zionist concept of the unity of Jewish people and their land, meaning Palestine. The Dutch Reformed Church went even further than the Declaration of the State of Israel by declaring this unity of the "Jewish people" and Palestine not as a matter of natural or historic right, but rather as a matter of divine covenant grounded in the promise of land to Abraham. It was a *novum* in church documents to have a section entitled "The State of Israel." The "return of the Jews to settle on the land" gives, so the document declared, the Jewish people a concrete and visible form that was interpreted by the document's authors as a "sign of God's protective faithfulness," and is interpreted theologically as a matter of salvation history.[15] The document stops short of bestowing divine qualities on the State of Israel but implies a historical necessity, albeit with a faith dimension.

In 1980, the General Synod of the Evangelical Church in Rheinland (EKiR) adopted a resolution for the renewal of the relationship between Christians and Jews.[16] Four reasons made this resolution a necessity according to the synod of the EKiR: first, the realization of Christian responsibility and guilt in the persecution and murdering of Jews during Nazi Germany leading to the Holocaust; second, new biblical insights by the confessing church of the permanent importance of "Israel" in salvation history; third, the insight that the ongoing existence of the Jewish people, their "return" to the land of promise, and the establishment of the State of Israel is a sign of God's faith-

[15]Ibid.

[16]Katja Kriener and Johann Michael Schmidt, *Gottes Treue—Hoffnung von Christen und Juden. Die Auseinandersetzung um die Ergänzung des Grundartikels der Kirchenordnung der Evangelischen Kirche im Rheinland* (Neukirchen-Vluyn, Germany: Neukirchener Theologie, 1998), 24.

fulness to God's people; fourth, the readiness of Jews to enter into dialogue with Christians, and to learn and work together in spite of the Holocaust.

Two elements: "unity of God, land, and people" and the "theological attribute to the State of Israel" became important features of Protestant liberal theologies of the 1970s and 1980s. We find these concepts used in different shades by theologians like Hendrikus Berkhof in Holland; Helmut Gollwitzer, Friedrich Wilhelm Marquardt, Rolf Rendtorff, Peter von der Osten-Sacken, and Bernhard Klappert in Germany; and Paul van Buren, Franklin Littell, Roy Eckardt, and W. D. Davies in the United States. Catholics, too, advanced these theologies through the work of individuals like the French philosopher Jacques Maritain and theologians like Kurt Hruby, Clemens Thoma, and Franz Mussner. Almost all of these theologians were influenced by Christian Holocaust theology and are considered to be liberal Christian Zionists who attempted to resurrect liberal Protestant and Catholic support for Israel.[17]

One of the most prominent German liberal Christian Zionists was Friedrich Wilhelm Marquardt. In his book *The Jews and Their Land*, written immediately after the 1967 war, Marquardt tried to prove that the land (Palestine) plays an important role in the New Testament and in the life of Jesus.[18] Marquardt moves on to speak about the importance of the State of Israel for Christians. Interestingly, he praises Balfour's *realpolitik* that was interwoven with "real religiosity"—in other words, Balfour's Christian Zionism. This "spirit of political and biblical realism" means for contemporary Christians nothing less than to stand for the "righteousness of Israel's claims" and for the "assertion

---

[17]Stephen R. Haynes, "Christian Holocaust Theology: A Critical Reassessment," *Journal of the American Academy of Religion* 62, no. 2 (1994): 562.

[18]Friedrich Wilhelm Marquardt, *Die Juden Und Ihr Land* (Gütersloh, Germany: Guetersloher Verlagshaus, 1993).

of Jews," Marquardt claimed.[19] No wonder that Marquardt titled his Christology *The Confession to Jesus, the Jew.*[20] In a lecture given at the Kirchtag in 1969, Marquardt went further and stated that the State of Israel was the bearer and fulfiller of God's promises, and has the potential to realize the Kingdom of God for Israel and the nations on earth.[21] Therefore, he continued, it is obligatory for Christians to fight for the rights of the State of Israel, not only for political calculations but also from theological conviction.

On the American continent, the most prominent American liberal Christian Zionist theologian was, no doubt, Paul van Buren. Like Marquardt, he was a student of Karl Barth, and in 1984, he published his volume on *A Christian Theology of the People of Israel.*[22] Van Buren asserts the exclusivity of God's covenant with Israel. The covenant implied a promised land that is given to "Israel" eternally, irrespective of whether the Jews live on the land or in exile, and irrespective of other people living there. The Jewish presence on the land takes the form of a state where Jews alone are full citizens and where strangers are tolerated as long as they observe the same laws as the Jews. Furthermore, the state is mandated by God to be a theocratic state under the Torah. For Van Buren, there is no doubt that the theological qualities of the State of Israel are not only for Jews since Israel is also the beginning of the redemption of all of creation.

The role of the Christian church is to extend the revelation of the God of Israel—and the healing work of God

---

[19]Ibid., 144–47.

[20]Friedrich-Wilhelm Marquardt, *Das christliche Bekenntnis zu Jesus, dem Juden.: Eine Christologie. Band 1+2. Studienausgabe* (Kamen, Germany: Hartmut Spenner, 2013).

[21]Kickel, *das gelobte Land*, 192–94.

[22]Paul M. Van Buren, *A Christian Theology of the People of Israel* (New York: Harper San Francisco, 1984).

in and through Israel—to the nations. Christianity should do this, not only by preaching this gospel to the nations, but also by rendering service to the people of Israel. This service takes an external and internal form. Externally, the Christian church must become the extension of the Anti-Defamation League, combating all anti-Semitism among Gentiles. It also takes the form of defense of the State of Israel, both raising money for Israel's defense and defending the State of Israel against all anti-Zionist calumny. All criticism of the State of Israel, whether based on alleged injustice to the Palestinians or claims that Israel is unjust to Third World peoples, are simply lies. It is the job of the Christian church to combat all these lies against Israel, being taught the truth by Jews; that is, the government of the State of Israel.[23]

Both Van Buren and Marquardt speak bluntly and unapologetically of the Christian duty to lobby on behalf of the State of Israel. The two church statements said the same in a more subtle way. Almost all of these theologians went even further by attacking and defaming those who dared to raise the question of justice for the Palestinians, including Rosemary Radford Ruether, a liberal Catholic theologian who used to be their ally and published explicitly against anti-Semitism. However, when she and her husband wrote *The Wrath of Jonah*, exposing, among other things, the danger of liberal Christian Zionism, she was attacked vigorously by these same theologians who, in turn, charged her with being anti-Semitic.[24] The accusation of anti-Semitism is used over and over again by the State of Israel

[23]Paul van Buren as quoted in Rosemary Radford Ruether, *The Wrath of Jonah: The Crisis of Religious Nationalism in the Israeli-Palestinian Conflict* (San Francisco: Harper & Row, 1989), 212.
[24]Haynes, "Christian Holocaust Theology," 569.

to silence critical voices and to assassinate the character of individuals who speak up against their settler colonial project.

By emphasizing the unity of people, land, and God's covenant, the two churches and theologians adopted a settler colonial discourse that supported the "return" and settlement of the Jews in Palestine. They constructed the Jews as the rightful owners of Palestine and the Palestinians as strangers in their own land. Palestinians remain invisible or are portrayed as savage people who "stand in God's way." The metanarrative for the post-Holocaust churches and theologians was, without doubt, the Holocaust, with its legacy of guilt and shame. For these liberal Christian Zionists, the Holocaust required a radical and a nonconventional theological response.

However, glocal considerations play a role in all cases. For the Dutch Reformed Church, two considerations were important: the strong resistance movement in the Netherlands against the German occupation created a special emotional bond with Israel, and the Dutch Reformed Church had a long tradition of support for the settler colonial project in South Africa, giving vehement backing to the Apartheid system there. For the EKiR, German guilt and the need for reparation for what happened to the Jews in Nazi Germany and by the official German church drove their policies. Marquardt himself served as a young soldier in the Nazi army in Poland. Liberal Christian Zionist theologians forged careers on the back of post-Holocaust theology and on the backs of indigenous Palestinians.

Christian Zionism
and the American Christian Right

The State of Israel has played a prominent role in American culture over the past five decades. The 1967 war gave a boost to American Christian Zionism, and the branding of the State as "biblical Israel" accelerated after 1967. In the wake of countless US losses in Vietnam, Israel's victory over several Arab states was seen by many American conservative Christians as proof of Israel's divine election and as an American jeremiad.[25] Inspired by the 1967 war, Hal Lindsey published in 1970 *The Late Great Planet Earth,* in which he claimed that all biblical prophecies showed that the end of "history as we know it" was near and, thus, the Second Coming was nigh, with a special place for the State of Israel in these unfolding events.[26] The book became a bestseller, selling over twenty-eight million copies.

The year when the Likud party came to power in Israel, 1977, was an important moment in the development of American Christian Zionism.[27] Likud, along with the National Religious Party, have much in common with American Christian Zionists. They believe that all of historic Palestine must be part of the State of Israel. Menachim Begin was one of the first Likud leaders to understand the importance of utilizing Christian Zionists as lobbyists for Israeli interests, and he was followed by Shiranski, Netanyahu, Ben Ayalon, and others.[28] At this stage, Christian Zionists had a direct connection to the Israeli political establishment. They launched huge programs to support the so-called *aliyah,* bringing Jews from several countries, such as the Soviet Union and Ethiopia, to Israel, and to boost Christian tourism to Israel, coinciding yearly since 1979 with the Feast of Tabernacles. When the Israeli Knesset passed a law declaring Jerusalem to be the eternal capital of Israel in 1980, all embassies moved their staff to Tel Aviv. That same year, and

---

[25]Andrew R. Murphy, *Prodigal Nation: Moral Decline and Divine Punishment from New England to 9/11* (Oxford: Oxford University Press, 2008).

[26]Hal Lindsey and Carole C. Carlson, *The Late Great Planet Earth* (Grand Rapids: Zondervan Academic, 1970).

[27]Goran Gunner, "Palestinian Christian Reflection on Christian Zionism," in *Comprehending Christian Zionism: Perspectives in Comparison* (Minneapolis: Fortress Press, 2014), 191–98.

[28]http://www.historycommons.org/entity.jsp?entity=menachem_begin.

to recognize Jerusalem as the eternal capital of Israel, a group of Christian Zionists created the International Christian Embassy in Jerusalem.[29] Bestselling novels in this era included a series of Christian dispensationalist literature entitled *Left Behind*, published between 1995 and 2000 and centering Jerusalem amid an end-of-time apocalypse.[30]

The War on Terror under the second Bush administration further strengthened the bond between the State of Israel and the United States, but the Trump era gave the Christian Zionist movement its most significant political support when the administration moved the US Embassy to Jerusalem, recognized the city as the capital of Israel, declared Jewish settlements in the West Bank as legal, and recognized the occupied Golan Heights as part of Israel. It should be no wonder, then, that two of the most prominent American Christian Zionists were invited to the opening of the US Embassy in Jerusalem and asked to say prayers at the event.

The first prayer was made by John Hagee, the founder and senior pastor of Cornerstone Church and the founder and national president of Christians United for Israel, a nonprofit organization incorporated in 2006 that boasts of having raised over one hundred million dollars in support for Israel. The second was Pastor Robert Jeffress, pastor of the First Baptist Church in Dallas and a televangelist. After the opening of the embassy, Netanyahu had a private talk with both pastors and asked them to lobby Latin American countries to follow Trump's lead and move their embassies to Jerusalem. American Christian Zionist leaders also lobbied the Gulf countries to open diplomatic relations with Israel.[31]

---

[29]https://int.icej.org.

[30]Tim LaHaye and Jerry B. Jenkins, *Left Behind: A Novel of the Earth's Last Days* (Chicago: Tyndale House Publishers, 1995).

[31]Joel C. Rosenberg, "First-Ever Delegation of Evangelical Leaders Visits United Arab Emirates," Joel C. Rosenberg's Blog, October 31, 2018, http://flash trafficblog.allisrael.com/2018/10/31/first-ever-delegation-of-evangelical-leaders-

Today, American Christian Zionists are Israel's second strongest lobby after the American Israel Public Affairs Committee. They invest heavily in Israel's settler colonial project in the West Bank because the image of a settler has a special connotation in American minds. Both countries are settler colonial nations who occupied the lands of native people and pushed them into small reservations. Vice President Pence makes the connection clear in his speech at the Knesset in 2018:

> In the story of the Jews, we've always seen the story of America. It is the story of an exodus, a journey from persecution to freedom, a story that shows the power of faith and the promise of hope. My country's very first settlers also saw themselves as pilgrims, sent by Providence, to build a new Promised Land.[32]

Pence spells out the whole ideology of settler colonialism. For him, Palestine does not exist, and the land belongs to the Jews by divine decree.

The metanarrative of the American Christian Right is American nationalism.[33] American nationalism can take several forms, from American imperialism to anticommunism, from anti-Muslim ideologies to American exceptionalism. As Braden Anderson writes, the American Christian Right views

> America as the New Israel or less directly, as a divinely elect nation of the contemporary world chosen to save

---

visits-united-arab-emirates-we-thanked-crown-prince-for-his-protection-of-freedom-of-worship-for-churches-and-for-his-moral-clarity-in-countering-violent/.

[32]"Full Transcript of Pence's Knesset Speech—The Jerusalem Post," January 23, 2018, https://www.jpost.com/Israel-News/Full-transcript-of-Pences-Knesset-speech-539476.

[33]Braden P. Anderson, *Chosen Nation* (Eugene, OR: Cascade Books, 2012), 150–97.

the world via its politics, economics, and culture as well as its own innate moral goodness, provided it stays true to its true self. These narratives interweave elements of the biblical narrative with those of American history and myth, resulting in a syncretized nationalist narrative of American chosenness that equates faithfulness to America with faithfulness to Jesus Christ, thus making American national identity a gospel imperative.[34]

Trump's America First priorities were meant to cater to this specific constituency. American Christian Zionists also have glocal considerations. Their main goal is to restore the Christian character of American culture in the face of secularism and to provide conservative Christian-based values and solutions to America's social problems in the face of sweeping liberalism. Israel serves them well in this agenda as a proof of the validity of the biblical story and their dispensationalist agenda.

Conclusion

Christian Zionism is a multifaceted phenomenon. It cannot be confined to evangelicals or dispensationalists, since it is found in different shades among political actors, liberal theologians, and mainline churches. While the theological rationale varies from one group to another, what they have in common is an undifferentiated use of the word *Israel*. All Christian Zionists confuse the Israelites of the Bible with Israelis today, thereby developing an emotional attachment to Jews in general, and the State of Israel in particular. For them, the Palestinian people are invisible or part of the problem.

Christian Zionism has to be understood as a religious lobby

---

[34]Ibid., 250–51.

in support of the last active settler colonial enterprise and the longest occupation in modern history. It weaponizes the Bible for an imperial Western project intended to eliminate the native people while confiscating their land and exploiting their resources. Because it is embedded within metanarratives and intertwined with several glocal agendas beyond Palestine, Christian Zionism is dangerous to Palestinians and Palestinian land. According to international law, the International Court of Justice, the Geneva Convention, and the Human Rights Charter, Israel's settler colonial project is illegal and violates laws and rights. It is condemned by most countries. B'Tselem, a Jewish human rights organization, was the first to describe what is happening in Israel as apartheid.[35] Under these circumstances, it has become more and more difficult to defend the settlement project of Israel. However, Christian Zionists disregard the Human Rights Charter because "biblical rights" supersede all other rights. In such a context, Christian Zionists might be Israel's last allies for its settler colonial enterprise. They may be the only group outside of the Israeli political and religious right that defends, supports, and promotes such Israeli violations.

Christian Zionism today is no longer a Western phenomenon. The Israeli government promotes Christian Zionist allies as the sole voice of Christianity abroad through continuous attempts to silence the voice of native Palestinian Christian leaders and replace it with that of Christian Zionists. The American empire and Western theologians have exported this ideology to the Global South. Christian Zionism is a growing phenomenon in African, Asian, and Latin American countries, a phenomenon that is intertwined with populism, religious nationalism, Islamophobia, and White supremacy.[36] In the last few years, we

---

[35]https://www.btselem.org/apartheid.
[36]Cynthia Holder Rich, ed., *Christian Zionism in Africa* (Lanham, MD: Fortress Academic, 2021); Hatem Bazian, "Understanding Christian Zionism

have even begun to see Christian Zionism beyond Christianity as the American empire spreads. Here, I reference the first signs of what we might call Islamic Zionism, a brand of Islam that is promoted by the Gulf rulers to support their normalization efforts with Israel. The imperial project that started in the mid-nineteenth century is continuing today.

A Special Report by the Islamophobia Studies Center," Islamophobia Studies Center, 2020, https://www.academia.edu/44030879/Understanding_Christian_Zionism_A_Special_Report_by_the_Islamophobia_Studies_Center.

3

The Land, the Bible, and Settler Colonialism

When Christian pilgrims visit Palestine, many want to reinvent the Holy Land of the Bible. They are excited about how the Bible comes alive in Palestine. Similarly, nineteenth-century archeologists digging in Palestine were looking for the Bible, and theologians today continue this search. As the previous chapter discussed, many Christian theologians write about Palestine from minds that are colonized with the Bible and a Westernized narrative. They write as if Palestine were an ancient land that exists in a vacuum; they strip it of its sociopolitical context—of its real people—and they rarely think about how this theology has and is being used to enhance settler colonialism. These colonized minds reinforce the continuing colonization of Palestine. This chapter focuses on these connections. The reference to the Temple Mount is an important example of such colonial discourse.

The Haram versus Temple Mount

A few years ago, I wanted to publish a book on Jerusalem. To that end, I approached a good friend, a theologian from the

United States, to work with me on this book. When we met to discuss the table of contents and topics, it became clear to me that we had two very different perspectives on Jerusalem. For me, Jerusalem was a real city that I used to visit as a boy on a weekly basis. I still vividly recall how I used to sit with my friends on the Ottoman walls of the Old City; visit the Church of the Holy Sepulcher, which dates back in part to the Byzantine era; and walk to the al-Aqsa Mosque and the Dome of the Rock, built during the Ummayyad period in the seventh century. A trip to Jerusalem was never complete without buying the famous Jerusalem *ka'ek*, a local bread with sesame seeds, and eating it with *za'atar* (wild thyme). I had an aunt and many friends from the church youth group who lived in Jerusalem. For me, Jerusalem was a vibrant, living city with real people.

My colleague from the United States did not have the same connection to the city, and I soon came to realize that he was not particularly interested in the city as it is today. Rather, he was obsessed with ancient Jerusalem, with what once existed, and that alone colonized his imagination. He was intrigued by the remains of the Herodian walls and paid little attention to the existing Ottoman wall from the sixteenth century. He concentrated on the ancient roads on which Jesus walked rather than the current *souq* with its rich social and economic history. He was intrigued by the Second Temple and was less interested in the al-Aqsa Mosque that has been standing since the seventh century. He was less interested in the city as it is and as it has developed over the centuries, focusing clearly on biblical Jerusalem, the Jerusalem of the Old and the New Testament. My friend was eager to reinvent the Jerusalem of the Bible and to bring it back to life for the potential readers of the planned book. His focus on the biblical past would not have been a problem but for the devastating consequences such focus has for current realities in Palestine. My friend was not a Zionist or evangelical Christian but was a sophisticated theologian raised in a liberal environment of historical criticism. Indeed, he may not have even recognized how his focus served as a tool in the continuing colonization of Palestinian land and people.

I recognized his focus on the biblical Jerusalem in his language. He referred to the area of the al-Aqsa Mosque and the Dome of the Rock (the Haram) as the "Temple Mount." Why would a Christian theologian call this area the Temple Mount when there has not been a temple there for the last two thousand years, and two major and ancient Muslim shrines dominate the skyline? The phrase *Temple Mount* is understandably used as a historical reference to where the Jewish Temple might once have stood or as an archeological reference to some of the remains of the Herodian wall. Yet ignoring and failing to reference two current and major Muslim holy sites, instead referring to the whole area as the Temple Mount, can no longer be understood as innocent. In today's volatile political context, the very phrase is problematic, to say the least.

The use of the term *Temple Mount* plays into the agenda of a radical (Christian) Zionist ideology as well as settler colonialism. Christian theologians are often unaware that Zionist political claims lay behind the phrase *Temple Mount*, and using the term innocently often panders to radical Israeli settlers who are determined to colonize the Muslim shrines and turn them into a Jewish site. Over the past five decades, Israeli settlers have attempted to destroy or occupy the Haram in order to construct a Jewish temple there. This is the current *Sitz im Leben* of this term.

Following the Israeli occupation of East Jerusalem, an Israeli military officer, Gershom Salomon, founded an organization named Temple Mount Faithful with the goal of "building the Third Temple on the Temple Mount in Jerusalem in our lifetime in accordance with the Word of G-d and all the Hebrew Prophets, and the liberation of the Temple Mount from Arab (Islamic) occupation so that it may be consecrated to the Name of G-d."[1] On August 21, 1969, a militant Christian Zionist and Australian citizen, Michael Dennis Rohan, set fire to the ancient pulpit commissioned by Salah ad-Din in the al-Aqsa Mosque in the belief that he had been called to burn the Muslim shrine so the Jewish Temple could be erected there.[2] Rohan was declared insane and later deported to Australia. Christian Zionist groups remain obsessed with the idea of seeing the third temple constructed, the Muslims defeated, and their shrines in Jerusalem destroyed as a prerequisite for the second coming of Christ.[3]

Starting in the late 1970s, Jewish terrorist groups attempted several times to blow up the Dome of the Rock. The first attempt took place in 1978 by Yehuda Etzion, who believed that the destruction of the Muslim mosque would trigger a Jewish national spiritual revival.[4] He and another Israeli-Jewish terrorist and expert in explosives, Menachem Livni, studied the Haram in detail, stole explosives from an Israeli military base in the Golan Heights, and made twenty-eight precision bombs to blow up the Dome of the Rock. For several reasons, the operation had to be postponed. A second attempt to blow up the Dome of the Rock occurred in 1980 at the hands of an American-Israeli rabbi and Member of the Knesset, Meir Kahane, followed by a third attempt in 1982 by Alan Goodman, an Orthodox Jewish American who opened fire at Muslim worshipers.[5] By the mid-1980s, attempts to storm the Haram by Jewish settlers had become a regular practice.

---

[1]"Temple Mount & Land of Israel Faithful Movement," www.templemount faithful.org.

[2]David S. New, *Holy War: The Rise of Militant Christian, Jewish, and Islamic Fundamentalism* (Jefferson, NC: McFarland, 2002), 154.

[3]Grace Halsell, "Militant Coalition of Christian Fundamentalist and Jewish Orthodox Cults Plots Destruction of Al Aqsa Mosque," March 14, 2000, https://www.wrmea.org/000-march/militant-coalition-of-christian-fundamentalist-and-jewish-orthodox-cults-plots-destruction-of-al-aqsa-mosque.html.

[4]New, *Holy War*, 155.

[5]Ibid.

During the First Intifada (uprising), Gershom Salomon, the leader of the Temple Mount Faithful, announced his intention to storm the Haram area and lay the foundation for the new temple. In 1996, Netanyahu's government authorized the opening of a tunnel underneath the Haram, giving new momentum to the Temple Mount Faithful movement. Gershom Salomon was proud to announce his goal: "We will liberate the Temple Mount, even if the political leadership doesn't want to . . . Instead of the Dome of the Rock and mosques, the flag of Israel and the Temple! . . . It's the will of Providence that we struggle to remove the abominations from the Mount."[6] On September 29, 2000, Israeli opposition leader Ariel Sharon, guarded by Israeli soldiers and accompanied by members of the Israeli government, stormed the Haram, an event that triggered the Second Intifada.[7] Such attempts have continued since then on an almost weekly basis, provoking Muslim worshipers and authorities, and leading to riots and the deaths of hundreds of Palestinians.

With a history of Jewish settler colonialism that resembles the acts of the Crusaders, theologians cannot employ the term *Temple Mount* in innocence. The crucial question for theology must be "How can we liberate theological minds from this invisible 'colonization'?" It is time to break away from language that plays into the hands of Jewish settler colonialism, Christian Zionist ideology, and Islamophobic rhetoric. What is true for the al-Aqsa Mosque is true for the entire land. How we name things is important, for naming is an exercise of power.

---

[6]Ibid., 160.

[7]Joel Greenberg, "Sharon Touches a Nerve, and Jerusalem Explodes," *New York Times*, September 29, 2000.

The Land Named Canaan

The oldest name of the land was Canaan. This ancient name referred to Southwest Asia, an area covering today's Palestine, Lebanon, and the western parts of Jordan and coastal Syria. The continuity of the Canaanite population is traced by scholars back to the eighth millennium BC.[8] Archeological remains from the Early Bronze Age II-III (3200–2200 BC) reveal a flourishing society capable of constructing massive structures, especially temples, to which further fortifications and palaces were added in the Middle Bronze Age (1800–1550 BC). During this period, Canaan enjoyed a period of relative autonomy and prosperity. The first textual and historical evidence of Canaan dates from around 1800 BC, one millennium older than the oldest biblical text. In the Late Bronze Age (1550–1200 BC), the land came under Egyptian rule, and the earliest textual references from this era refer to Canaan as a distinct geopolitical entity in the region. This is corroborated in the Amarna letters written by Canaanite rulers in Akkadian script on clay tablets between 1360 and 1332 BC, where Canaan and the Canaanites are mentioned twelve times. These letters give an impression of a distinct West Semitic Canaanite dialect and an agrarian lifestyle in which local rulers governed small areas with a large, walled city at the center.[9] Their most important deities were El, Baal, and Asherah with their focus on fertility, which constituted a crucial element for their agrarian society with its dependence on rain.

The Old Testament does not shy away from calling the land by its ancient name of Canaan, and its inhabitants as Canaanites,

---

[8]Jonathan N. Tubb, *Canaanites*, Illustrated ed. (Norman: University of Oklahoma Press, 1999), 13–14.

[9]Mary Ellen Buck, *The Canaanites: Their History and Culture from Texts and Artifacts* (Eugene, OR: Cascade Books, 2019), 30–55.

on over 150 occasions. The biblical text testifies to the advanced culture of the "land of milk and honey" (Joshua 5:6). The name Canaan and its peoples, the Canaanites, remained in use way into the fifth century AD. The gospel of Matthew 15:22 written in the late first century AD refers to a Syro-Phoenician woman (Mark 7:26) as a Canaanite, while the last reference to the Canaanites is by St. Augustine of Hippo in his commentary on Romans 13. Although the names Canaan and Canaanites disappeared, the Canaanites themselves did not. They continued to be the people inhabiting Palestine but with new identities. The biblical narrative that stereotypes the Canaanite as cursed (Genesis 9:25) may have contributed to this process. In modern times and in the context of the Israeli–Palestinian struggle for historicity and legitimacy as the owners of the land, some Palestinian groups and intellectuals started referring to the Canaanites as their ancestors who preceded the Israelites. This identification is problematic and does not take into consideration elements of history, which leads to a distorted vision. The Palestinians of today are not the Canaanites, but Canaanites are without doubt part of Palestinian ancestry.

Palestine

The transition from the Late Bronze Age to the Iron Age I (1200–950 BC) is marked by the appearance of the Sea People, with their new and advanced iron weaponry on the southern and western shores of the Mediterranean, resulting in a new configuration of the region. The Peleset, known as the Philistines, who settled permanently on the southern coastal area of Canaan, were one group of the most famous Sea People. A weakened Egypt had to withdraw from Canaan, and localized kingdoms known as the Phoenicians, Israelites, Moabites, Ammonites, and Edomites were able to fill the vacuum.

The emergence of Philistia on the southeastern side of the Mediterranean was a defining moment, and Palestine became the name used most consistently since the Iron Age to refer to the area stretching from as far north as Sidon to the Brook of Egypt, and from the Mediterranean into Transjordan with ever-changing borders. It is seen in inscriptions from Ramses III (ca. 1182–1151) with increased regional comprehension in the twelfth and tenth centuries BC. From the neo-Assyrian period (tenth through seventh centuries BCE) onward, it is the most common etic collective designation, also appearing in the Roman period (first century BC through fourth century CE).[10]

While the Assyrians, already under Ramses III, used the name in the form of Pilishtu to describe the coastal region of the land, it was the Greek historiographer and cartographer Herodotus (ca. 484–425 BC) who recrafted the term to become Palaistin, referring to the entire land, including even Transjordan.[11] With the exception of Canaan, no other name for this land but Palestine has been used continuously for almost 2,500 years, up to the present day. In addition, only this name has historically had an inclusive character. Palestine in this sense does not refer to a political, religious, or ethnic entity, but rather to a multiethnic, multicultural, and multireligious region that was able to include diverse identities and peoples within its boundaries. During these 2,500 years, Palestine stood for a land with an inclusive, multireligious society. The Palestinians of today are not the Philistines of the Bible, although the Philistines are a feature of Palestinian ancestry.

---

[10]Ingrid Hjelm, "The Palestine History and Heritage Project (PaHH)," in *The Ever Elusive Past: Discussions of Palestine's History and Heritage* (United Arab Emirates: Dar Al Nasher, 2019), 11.

[11]Nur Masalha, *Palestine: A Four-Thousand-Year History* (London: Zed Books, 2018), 72–73.

Israel

Israel was another kingdom that surfaced on the land during Iron Age I. While the biblical story describes them as coming from Egypt following the exodus, most historians today believe that they were seminomadic tribes that regrouped as a result of the Egyptian withdrawal from Canaan to establish a new kingdom in the highlands with a new religious identity focused on Jahwe.[12] Their seminomadic background must have brought them into a direct clash with the Baal religion centered on the fertile regions of Palestine.

The Bible ascribes the establishment of Israel as a political entity in Palestine to King David and his son Solomon, who may have lived in Canaan in the Iron Age I period, around 1000 BC. The biblical story retroactively glorified the time of David and Solomon as the climax of "Israel." This story has been weaponized by Jewish Zionists and Christian Zionists as the historical reference for the settler colonial narrative and practice. Interestingly, there are no historical or archeological records that correspond to the biblical story of David. Most probably, David was a guerilla fighter from Judah who rendered and sold his fighting services, and who was able to take over the twelve-acre Canaanite city of Jebus with its couple-of-thousand Jebusite population and transform it into his political base. This

---

[12]Three theories were developed about the origin of ancient Israel. The American School of Biblical Archeology, represented by William Albright and John Bright, defended the conquest theory by stating that the conquest under Joshua was real. The German school of Albrecht Alt and Martin Noth, on the other hand, advocated the peaceful infiltration theory, meaning that the Israelites were nomads from outside who infiltrated Palestine and settled there peacefully. A third school, represented by George Mendenhall and Norman Gottwald, argued for a peasants' revolt model, saying that the Israelites were Canaanite peasants who revolted against the existing sociopolitical and economic structures of their time and retreated to the Highlands to form a new society.

small territory with a few hundred fighters was short lived, but the biblical story refers to it and to the period of Solomon as if it were an imperial power controlling all of Palestine.[13]

Historically speaking, the name Israel referred mainly to the north of the land during a relatively short period of time known as the Kingdom of Israel or House of Omri (tenth century to 720 BC). This region was later called Samaria, and was distinct and at odds with the south, called Judea. The term *Land of Israel* took root in rabbinic Judaism only after the destruction of the Temple in 586 BC. These roots contextualize the singular occurrence of the phrase in scripture, in Matthew 2:21. Thus, although the name Israel referring to the Northern Kingdom disappeared, Israel as a theological concept did not and survived throughout the biblical story. It is, therefore, imperative to distinguish between history and the biblical story, between Israel as a name of the Northern Kingdom and between Israel as a theological concept referring to the "people of God." In turn, both usages must be distinguished from the contemporary State of Israel.

The name Israel was chosen in the twentieth century by a modern political entity, the "State of Israel," which projected an exclusive ethno-national and religious state into the Bible, now used by the current Israeli government as a pretext for land colonization.[14] However, the Christian or rabbinic incarnation of the term is not identical in meaning to the term employed in the context of the Jewish connection to the territory in a modern age of nationalism. Only in the early twentieth century, after years in the Protestant melting pot, was the theological concept of the Land of Israel refined into a geonational concept. Settle-

---

[13]Samuel Pagan, "The Theological and Historical David: Contextual Reading," in *The Biblical Text in the Context of Occupation: Towards a New Hermeneutics of Liberation*, ed. Mitri Raheb (Bethlehem: Diyar, 2012), 336–40.

[14]More on these three different uses of the word *Israel* can be found in Philip R. Davies, *In Search of "Ancient Israel": A Study in Biblical Origins*, 2nd ed. (New York: T&T Clark, 2015).

ment Zionism borrowed the term from rabbinic tradition in part to displace the term *Palestine*, which was widely used at the time not only throughout Europe but also by all of the first-generation Zionist leaders. In the new language of the settlers, the Land of Israel became the exclusive name of the region.[15]

Naming is a means to exercise power, to claim dominance over land and people, and it constitutes an important aspect of settler colonial projects. After conquering Carthage, the Romans coined the word *Africa* to refer to the conquered region, a name that was later expanded to refer to the whole continent. A Spanish conqueror renamed Anahuac as America. By evoking a biblical name, Israel, for a modern state in 1948, Jewish European settlers instrumentalized an ancient biblical story for the creation of a new exclusive national identity, while at the same time erasing the name Palestine and marginalizing its indigenous people—another important element of settler colonial practice. Four hundred and fifty-two Palestinian villages were erased from the map as if they never existed, with just the cactus trees remaining as the witnesses to this ethnic cleansing. Throughout the past seventy-five years, the State of Israel has erased as many Arabic names as possible, replacing them with Jewish and, often, biblical names. This act is intended to erase the indigenous history of the land and the identity of its native people.

Taken at face value and detached from history, the biblical story leads automatically to tunnel vision. Christians acquainted with the biblical story confuse it with history and subconsciously side with the State of Israel in seeing Palestinians as intruders on the land. Israeli settlers are often seen by Christians as the legal heirs to the land while the native Palestinians are the strangers. Some Jewish Israelis and Palestinians have Israelite ancestry, but the struggle today is one of identity. The biblical

---

[15]Shlomo Sand, *The Invention of the Land of Israel* (London: Verso, 2012), 28.

story that reflects the ancient identity of the peoples of the land is interpreted as an exclusive entitlement, and the Israelites of the Bible are confused with today's Israelis. The distortion of history and the instrumentalization of the biblical narrative by Zionism and Zionist Christians have dire consequences for the Palestinian people.

The Biblical Story and Israeli Settler Colonialism

Distorting history to advance poor biblical interpretation leaves the settler colonial nature of the State of Israel unquestioned. Rather, the conquest of Palestine and the establishment of the State of Israel is perceived as fulfillment of the land promise and "a sign of God's faithfulness." It is celebrated as a modern miracle and as if it were a replay of the biblical conquest story under Joshua. The most important segment of the biblical story for Jewish and Christian Zionists, the Torah and book of Joshua frighteningly contain all of the elements of settler colonialism as a political practice.[16] The Israelites who crossed the Jordan into Canaan are seen as having a divine entitlement to the land. They are portrayed as belonging to the land and as the legitimate heirs while the natives are described as wicked and decadent (Genesis 9:25), needing to be replaced, displaced, and exterminated (Deuteronomy 7:2), and their native deity erased (Deuteronomy 12:2–3), with their conquered cities renamed

---

[16]For more on this issue, see Pekka Pitkänen, "Pentateuch–Joshua: A Settler-Colonial Document of a Supplanting Society," *Settler Colonial Studies* 4, no. 3 (2014): 245–76, https://doi.org/10.1080/2201473X.2013.842626; Pekka Pitkänen, "Settler Colonialism in Ancient Israel," August 1, 2020, https://www.academia.edu/31712835/Settler_Colonialism_in_Ancient_Israel; Pekka Pitkänen, "Reading Genesis–Joshua as a Unified Document from an Early Date: A Settler Colonial Perspective," *Biblical Theology Bulletin*, February 3, 2015, https://doi.org/10.1177/0146107914564822.

and reclaimed. The book of Joshua is the blueprint par excellence of a settler colonial ideology and theology.

While the biblical texts themselves are very troublesome, the manner in which they have been received is even more so. These biblical passages have been repeatedly used as justification for land grabs and colonization in Palestine and beyond. The Bible has been used as a tool for colonization since the sixteenth century. The land promise was used repeatedly as the pretext for land confiscation and colonization in North America, Africa, and Australia, to name a few. With the Bible as their weapon, settler colonialists robbed indigenous populations of their land and livelihood, slaughtering, expelling, or confining survivors to small territories called "reservations" in North America, "Bantustans" in South Africa, or "Area A" in Palestine. With the Bible as their weapon, settler colonialists let their might constitute what was right, legitimizing their exploitative conquest and colonization with scriptural language. With the Bible as their weapon, settler colonialists demonized indigenous populations while glorifying colonization as the civilization of the savage. Israel is no exception to this pattern and must be understood within this context of European settler colonization. When we talk today about land theology, we cannot ignore the European history of colonization or shy away from the colonialist reception history of the Bible.

The colonization of ancient Canaan by the Israelites was a topic of discussion in the newly established State of Israel in the second half of the twentieth century. David Ben Gurion, Israel's first prime minster, chose to use the book of Joshua to advance the settler colonial project.[17] In 1958, the tenth anniversary of the creation of the State of Israel, which resulted in the Palestinian *Nakba* or catastrophe, Ben Gurion assembled

---

[17]Rachel Havrelock, *The Joshua Generation: Israeli Occupation and the Bible* (Princeton, NJ: Princeton University Press, 2022), 97–161.

Israeli generals, politicians, archeologists, and biblical scholars to read and interpret the book of Joshua to theologically justify the ethnic cleansing of Palestinians in 1948, and to forge an Israeli identity and Jewish essence based on ethno-nationalism and militarism. For Ben Gurion, there was no other way for the Jewish diaspora to understand the essence of the book of Joshua with its focus on military conquest and land settlements.

> Occupation, settlement, tribe, nation—I doubt if a scattered and divided people that has no land and no independence could know the true meaning of these words and their full content. Those who do not engage in conquest cannot know what is involved in the act of conquest. It is the same thing with settlement. Only with the establishment of Israel in our generation did these abstract concepts assume skin, sinews, and flesh, so that we know their content and essence.[18]

The book of Joshua was also central for another Israeli general, Moshe Dayan. For Dayan, the real conquest and settlement of the land that resembled the conquest of Joshua did not take place in 1948 but under his leadership in the 1967 war. Dayan saw himself as the real modern Joshua. In his book *Living with the Bible*, Dayan wrote,

> We are the biblical generation of the settlement, following the Joshua conquest, and the helmet and sword are essential requirements. There will be no life for our children unless we dig shelters, and without the barbed wire fence and the machine-gun we shall be unable to build a home, plant a tree, pave a road and drill for water.[19]

---

[18]Ibid., 109.
[19]Moshe Dayan, *Living with the Bible* (New York: Bantam Books, 1979), 105.

Joshua was the role model for Ben Gurion, Dayan, and for the many Jewish Zionist settlers who saw the book as a blueprint for their settler colonial project and the ethnic cleansing of the Palestinian people. The climax of the Joshua interpretation was crafted by Rabbi Zvi Yehuda Kook (1890–1982) who understood settler colonialism as divinely ordered: "The conquest of the land of Israel in order to establish our rule in it is a divinely ordained war. . . . Joshua made it plain to the inhabitants of the land: this land is ours. It is under our sovereignty."[20]

These consecutive interpretations of the book have had a lasting imprint on Israeli society and Modern Hebrew as a language. The word for the Israeli occupation, *kibbush*, derives from Joshua's systemic war against the Canaanites in Joshua 18:1. The word for settlement, *nahalah*, is the root of today's term for Israeli settler colonies, *hitnahalut*, and for settlers, *mitnahalim*, as attested in Joshua 19:35. The linguistic borrowing of settler colonial concepts from the book of Joshua in Israeli society today "sets the stage for lived reality insofar as figuring the Jewish citizens of Israel as the reincarnation of Joshua's army exalts the male soldier while assigning to the Palestinians the role of the Canaanites."[21] In today's Jewish messianism, settler colonialism is no longer an imperial undertaking but a divine plan that sanctions a holy war and sanctifies military operations. When settler colonialism becomes a divine order, human rights or international law becomes irrelevant since God's laws triumph human laws.

Settler Colonialism: The Blind Spot of Land Theology

In 1977, the well-known American Old Testament scholar Walter Brueggemann published his book entitled *The Land*, a

---

[20]Havrelock, *The Joshua Generation*, 177.
[21]Ibid., 98.

typical book about biblical theology that influenced a whole
generation of American pastors and theologians. In this book,
Brueggemann responded to an emerging American context
where many people felt a "sense of being lost, displacement
and homelessness."[22] This existential and sociopsychological
yearning for a secure place led Brueggemann to claim that the
Land is the "central theme in biblical faith"[23] and is primarily
concerned "with the issue of being displaced and yearning for
a place."[24] Brueggemann described three important aspects of
the land: as a gift, a temptation, and a task. This emphasized
the dialectic between landlessness and landedness.[25]

In the preface of the second edition of the same book,
Brueggemann wrote about five major developments in Old Testament studies in 2002 that were not on his horizon at the time
of the initial writing in 1977. One of them was the following:

> The recognition that the claim of "promised land" in the
> Old Testament is not an innocent theological claim, but is
> a vigorous ideological assertion on an important political
> scale. This insight is a subset of ideology critique in the
> field that has emerged as a major enterprise only in the
> last decades. Perhaps the most important articulation in
> this matter is the recognition of Jon Levenson that Israel's
> tradition demonizes and dismisses the Canaanites as a
> parallel to the anti-Semitism that is intrinsic to the New
> Testament. That is, Israel's text proceeds on the basis of
> the primal promises of Genesis 12–36 to assume entitle-
> ment to the land without regard to any other inhabitants,
> including those who may have been there prior to Israel's

---

[22]Walter Brueggemann, *The Land: Place as Gift, Promise, and Challenge in Biblical Faith*, Overtures to Biblical Theology (Philadelphia: Fortress Press, 1977), 1.

[23]Ibid., 3.

[24]Ibid., 2.

[25]Ibid., xi.

emergence . . . The shortcoming in my book reflects my inadequate understanding at that time, but also reflects the status of most Old Testament studies at that time that were still innocently credulous about the theological importance of the land tradition in the Old Testament . . . Most recently scholarly attention has been given to the ongoing ideological force (and cost) of the claim of "promised land." On the one hand, this ideology of land entitlement . . . has served the ongoing territorial ambitions of the state of Israel, ambitions that, as I write (April 2002), are enacted in unrestrained violence against the Palestinian population.[26]

When Brueggemann wrote his first book on the land, he was forty-six years old. That book was his thirteenth, and he was in the middle of his career. Christian theologians and others were very naïve, very much influenced by the so-called Christian Holocaust Theology, and in awe of the State of Israel. Many went on to emphasize a strong bond between God, land (Palestine), and people (Jewish).[27] Brueggemann and many others of this era were what Stephen Haynes calls "liberal Christian Zionists."[28]

The second edition of Brueggemann's book came out when he was at the height of his career. The political situation had changed dramatically between 1977 and 2002, and the second edition was published in the context of the Second Palestinian Intifada. Israeli tanks had invaded most of the Palestinian towns, the Church of the Nativity was under siege by Israeli troops, and President Arafat was imprisoned in his compound. Yet, Brueggemann attributes his changed perception to the

---

[26]Ibid., xiii–ix.

[27]W. D. Davies, *The Territorial Dimension of Judaism* (Minneapolis: Fortress Press, 1991).

[28]Stephen R. Haynes, "Christian Holocaust Theology: A Critical Reassessment," *Journal of the American Academy of Religion* 62, no. 2 (1994): 562.

emergence of ideology critique, although ideological criticism emerged around the same time that his first edition was published. In his book on the land, Brueggemann was keen to be relevant to his American context and to relate the issues of land as gift, promise, and challenge to issues existing within the American context. He failed to appreciate how this theology was misused in the founding of his own country, the United States, where biblical land theology and ideology were used in the conquest of North America and the occupying of Native American lands. Brueggemann was focused on the Bible and not on biblical reception history. I do not want to question Brueggemann's innocence, and I am glad to see him confessing his naiveté, but did that confession lead him to altering his theology in any radical way? Unfortunately not. He continued to be a liberal Christian Zionist.

In 2015, Brueggemann published a booklet under the title *Chosen? Reading the Bible amid the Israeli-Palestinian Conflict.*[29] The opening of this book sounds promising as Brueggemann is open about a change in his convictions. His connection to Palestinian Christian theologians and Jewish American peace activists played a role in this conversion:

> My own convictions concerning this conflict, as those of many other people, have changed considerably over time, a change that I judge responsible in the face of changing political reality. Mindful of the long history of Christian anti-Semitism and the deep fissure of the Shoah, we have surely been right to give thanks for the founding of the state of Israel and the securing of a Jewish homeland. But the issues have altered dramatically as the state of Israel

---

[29]Walter Brueggemann, *Chosen? Reading the Bible amid the Israeli-Palestinian Conflict* (Louisville, KY: Westminster John Knox Press, 2015).

has developed into a major military power that continues administrative-military control of the Palestinian territories.[30]

But very soon after, theological claims related to Israeli settler colonialism troublingly resurface in the introduction to this booklet:

> In my own thinking, which is much influenced by my work as a Scripture scholar, I begin with a focus on the claim of Israel as God's chosen people. That conviction is not in doubt in the Bible. It is a theological claim, moreover, that fits with compelling persuasiveness with the reality of Jews in the wake of World War II and the Shoah. Jews were indeed a vulnerable people, whose requirement of a homeland was an overriding urgency. Like many Christians, progressive and evangelical, I was grateful (and continue to be so) for the founding and prospering of the state of Israel as an embodiment of God's chosen people. That much is expressed in my earlier book entitled *The Land*. I took "the holy land" to be the appropriate place for the chosen people of the Bible which anticipates the well-being of Israel that takes land and people together.[31]

Brueggemann unapologetically connects the biblical promise of the land with the notion of "God's chosen people," a theological phrase that is rooted in Christian-Zionist ideology rather than the Bible. Brueggemann then moves swiftly, perplexingly, and uncritically to connect these biblical topoi with modern Judaism and speaks about the State of Israel as "an embodiment of God's

---

[30]Ibid., ix–x.
[31]Ibid., xiv.

chosen people."[32] In his booklet, Brueggemann confuses Israel, meaning the Northern Kingdom, with Israel as a theological construct, and with the State of Israel of today.[33] Even when he appears to criticize the occupational policies of the State of Israel, Brueggemann immediately feels a need to express his unshakable support for it. He writes, "I have not changed my mind an iota about the status of Israel as God's chosen people or about urgency for the security and well-being of the state of Israel."[34] This is pure liberal Christian Zionism.

At the end of chapter 3 Brueggemann appears to contradict himself when he asks the question: Is today's Israel biblical Israel? To this, he answers,

Concerning any interpretive question, critical faith will resist a direct line from ancient text to contemporary claim. The land issue is no exception to that general rule for critical interpretation. Consequently, it is simply not credible to make any direct appeal from the ancient promises of land to the state of Israel. That is so for two reasons. First, much has happened between text and contemporary political practice that resists such innocent simplicity. Second, because the state of Israel, perhaps of necessity, has opted to be a military power engaged in power politics along with the other nation-states of the world, it cannot at the same time appeal to an old faith tradition in a persuasive way. Thus, the state of Israel can, like any nation-state, make

[32]Ibid.

[33]For more on this confusion, see Philip R. Davies, *In Search of "Ancient Israel": A Study in Biblical Origins*, 2nd ed. (New York: T&T Clark, 2015); Ingrid Hjelm et al., eds., *A New Critical Approach to the History of Palestine: Palestine History and Heritage Project 1* (London: Routledge, 2019); Andrew Mein and Claudia V. Camp, *History, Politics and the Bible from the Iron Age to the Media Age*, ed. James G. Crossley and Jim West, reprint ed. (New York: T&T Clark, 2018).

[34]Brueggemann, *Chosen?*, xvi.

its legitimate political claims and insist upon legitimate security. But appeals to the ancient faith traditions about land promise in order to justify its claims carries little conviction except for those who innocently and uncritically accept the authority of that ancient story.[35]

There seems to be a serious disconnect here. Brueggemann is not a naïve evangelical Christian and does not connect biblical Israel with the State of Israel directly but uses the Shoah and anti-Semitism as hermeneutical keys to bridge both entities. Brueggemann is not troubled at all by this kind of theology but is concerned because "the state of Israel has developed into a major military power that continues administrative-military control of the Palestinian territories."[36]

Based on his theological understanding of the biblical issue of the land, Brueggemann does not question Israel's "biblical" and "unconditional" entitlement to the land; he is only troubled by the way Israel treats the Palestinians. To that end, Brueggemann finds the Israel of today to be in a similar context to that of biblical Israel at the time of Ezra. Those coming "back" to the land are developing exclusionist theologies about the other. As a result, Brueggemann sees "the question of the other" as "the interpretive key to how to read the Bible. The other can be perceived, as in the Zionist perspective, as a huge threat to the security of the state and the well-being of the holy seed. Conversely, the other can be perceived as a neighbor with whom to work at shalom."[37] Rabbi Michael Lerner and editor of *Tikkun* magazine commends Brueggemann for his approach of loving "the stranger/the Other."[38] Yet I contend that, by describing

---

[35]Ibid., 37–38.
[36]Ibid., x.
[37]Ibid., 7.
[38]Michael Lerner in his endorsement of the booklet; ibid., cover page.

the Palestinians as the stranger or the other, Rabbi Lerner and Brueggemann dangerously reinforce the settler colonialist focus on the Bible that views the English or Russian Israeli settlers as the heirs to the land.

While both men are concerned about discrimination against Palestinians by the State of Israel, they discriminate against Palestinians theologically by calling them strangers despite the fact that Palestinians and their history, culture, and identity are deeply rooted in the land of Palestine. As a Palestinian whose roots are in this land, I hear the biblical call to be kind to the Israeli incomers, but I vehemently resist being called a stranger and being made an alien in my homeland or discriminated against politically by Israel or theologically by Christians or Jews. The othering of the indigenous people by calling them strangers is an important feature of settler colonialism in which the natives are extraneous and the settlers are cast as natives.

In chapter 3 of the booklet, Brueggemann returns to the issue of "holy" land and reiterates the words he wrote many years ago of the land as a "gift with strings attached."[39] He summarizes it in this way: "Thus, the land is *given (unconditionally)*, the land is *taken (by conquest and force),* and the land is *losable (if the Torah is not kept)."*[40] Brueggemann does not question that God gave Israel the land of Palestine; he takes the militant conquest of Joshua as a biblical given without connecting it to the history of colonization. The only problem he sees is that Israel does not keep the Torah, and the Torah is equated with the human rights charters of today.

As the settler colonization of Palestinian land reaches un-paralleled dimensions in the twenty-first century, equating recognizing Torah with recognizing international human rights law is unacceptable. Israeli colonies are spread throughout the

---

[39]Ibid., 28.
[40]Ibid., 32.

West Bank, isolating Palestinian areas like the South African Bantustans and US reservation system abroad. Settlers seize land and resources, subjugating the indigenous population to apartheid laws under a political matrix of total control. Today, Israel occupies Palestinian land, air, water, and even subterranean electromagnetic fields. The expansion of Israel settlement colonies in the West Bank makes the international community largely uneasy, for they violate international law, including the Geneva Convention and Human Rights Charter. Recognizing international legal arguments, the Israeli government turns to theological claims to biblical entitlement to the land of Palestine as a final resort. In so doing, they attempt to subvert the violations of "human rights" by appealing to "divine right."

Ignoring the reception history of land ideology in modern settler colonial history while writing about the land and the Bible is irresponsible at best. Focus on scripture that does not engage reception history or acknowledge the many ways that biblical writings have been used to justify colonial histories and actions reflects and implicitly strengthens the colonial process itself. Brueggemann sees the Christian anti-Semitism that led to the Holocaust in the West but does not see the colonial history of the Christian West while it is active in North America and Palestine today. Nowhere in the booklet does Brueggemann refer to the notion of colonialism and its connection to land theology. In his framework regarding the exclusion of Black Americans, women, and LGBTQ+ people, he never refers to indigenous people of his own continent. Why is the theology of conquest not questioned? Is Brueggemann, a descendant of a settler community, ignorant to the troubling history of the colonization of North America, especially the use of the Doctrine of Discovery to seize Native American land? How can his mind be so focused on the Bible that he does not seriously examine its use in history and today?

Brueggemann is not an exception among biblical scholars

and Christian theologians. Yet it remains incomprehensible to me that the occupation of Palestinian land is seen as biblical and salvation history rather than as part of modern European colonial history. It is disturbing when theologians ignore how biblical ideology is used as a political claim with major colonial consequences. How can somebody like Brueggemann continue to ignore the current context in which land theology is used for the colonization of Palestinian land?[41]

In contrast to Brueggemann's land theology, I would like to look briefly at another Western theologian of almost the same age as Brueggemann who reached a different reading and conclusion. Norman Habel, a Lutheran Australian Old Testament scholar, published a book in 1995 titled *The Land Is Mine: Six Biblical Land Ideologies.* As the title implies, Habel was already aware that land theology "employ[s] theological doctrines, traditions, or symbols to justify and promote the social, economic and political interests of a group within society."[42] In his 2018 booklet *Acknowledgement of the Land and Faith of Aboriginal Custodians after Following the Abraham Trail,*[43] Habel went a step further. He was aware that most land theologies are used by colonizers and ignore the perspective of the colonized. This was not merely a theoretical observation but a biographical experience. In the preface, Habel writes,

> I am a descendant of a Prussian migrant who can be compared to Abraham who moved from his homeland, Ur of the Chaldees, to the host country of Canaan. And the Aboriginal people of Canaan can be compared to the Aboriginal peoples in the land of Australia and other

---

[41]Ibid., 8, 12.

[42]Norman C. Habel, *The Land Is Mine: Six Biblical Land Ideologies*, Overtures to Biblical Theology. (Minneapolis: Fortress Press, 1995), 10.

[43]Norman C. Habel, *Acknowledgement of the Land and Faith of Aboriginal Custodians after Following the Abraham Trail* (Eugene, OR: Wipf and Stock, 2018).

countries . . . Recent generations of colonial readers have viewed the promised land tradition of the narrator of the Abraham trail as a divine justification for entry into so-called uncivilized lands of the New World: lands like Australia, America and South Africa.[44]

Habel learned through an Aboriginal elder, George Rosendale, to read land theology from the perspective of the colonized. He quotes George, saying,

> Little was said [by the missionaries] about the indigenous people of the land whom the Israelites conquered. No questions were asked about whether Joshua's scorched Earth policy was what God really wanted for the indigenous people. Today Joshua's mode of operation sounds to us very much like that of the British colonial conquerors. Did the British have to follow Joshua's way?[45]

Habel starts his booklet with Canaan, the original land of promise, "a host country whose indigenous inhabitants welcomed immigrants such as Abraham and helped them settle peacefully."[46] Habel is, unlike Brueggemann, very conscious of his context as a German settler. He acknowledges that his settler community has often "discounted the capacity of Aboriginal people"[47] who have been custodians of Australia for thousands of years, and have dismissed Aboriginal beliefs as paganism, demoting their rich spirituality.

For Habel, there are two different land theologies in the Old Testament: the first is represented by Abraham who understands

---

[44]Ibid., 7–8.
[45]Ibid., 12.
[46]Ibid., 14.
[47]Ibid., 67.

himself as a guest in Canaan, respects the faith of the indigenous people, and enters into a peaceful treaty with them; the second is represented by Joshua with its militant version of the promise. The latter "classical promised land ideology seems to reflect a bias based on a belief that one chosen people has a divine mandate to invade and possess a particular land and dispossess the indigenous inhabitants of that land as peoples without rights, peoples such as the Australian Aboriginal peoples."[48]

Habel concludes his booklet by urging the church and its theologians to grasp the Kairos moment, and to follow the model of Abraham by changing their theology, attitudes, and practice. He writes,

> Yes!
> IT IS TIME!
> In the light of the faith of Abraham,
>   the positive relationships between Abraham
>   and the indigenous custodians of Canaan,
>   including worship of El, the Creator Spirit of Canaan,
>   a covenant with the same Canaanite God,
>   a treaty in which this God, Abraham, the Canaanites
>   and the land of Canaan are partners,
> AND
> In the light of how Australian settlers, influenced by a promised land ideology,
>   dispossessed the indigenous custodians,
>   discounted their creation spirituality
>   and violated the land they held sacred.
> IT IS TIME
> For Christian churches
>   and the descendants of Christian settlers
>   to follow the precedent of Abraham,

---

[48]Ibid., 42.

to make a public acknowledgment,
a colonial confession,
AND
To promote a treaty process
that guarantees and respects the identity, rights,
sovereignty, country and spirituality
of the Aboriginal Peoples.[49]

Habel's approach here fundamentally differs from that of Brueggemann. Both use the Bible and both write land theology, but they arrive at different conclusions. The Bible contains several conflicting stories like those of Abraham and of Joshua. However, what we find says not so much about the Bible but more about each of us as readers. Brueggemann's "land" interpretation says more about his political convictions than about biblical theology, and the same is true for Habel. The Bible has both texts of liberation and texts of colonization. What do our minds focus on? What is our hermeneutical key: the Holocaust or colonialism? Our keys determine to a great extent how we interpret the Bible and our focus.

We cannot separate Israeli colonial policies in Palestine from modern European colonial history. In his comparative analysis of Native American and Palestinian literary production, Steven Salaita reaches the following conclusion:

The results of ethnic cleansing have been heartbreaking in the New World and Holy Land. It is important—perhaps even imperative—to use "New World" and "Holy Land" together with "ethnic cleansing" whenever we discuss either region. One can argue convincingly that were it not for the destruction of Native nations in North America, there would have been no destruction of Palestine. The same

---

[49]Ibid., 74.

is true of other colonial incursions: the British settlement of Australia, the French takeover of Algeria, the European scramble for Africa. Zionism, as a European phenomenon of philosophy and execution, was produced in a culture that conceptualized foreign settlement and population transfer as viable political solutions, especially where so-called "inferior" peoples were concerned. David Ben Gurion and other prominent Zionist leaders looked to the Euro-American conquest of Native lands as a source of inspiration.[50]

No one should be allowed to use "biblical rights" to violate human rights; not Jewish settlers, Israeli politicians, or naïve Christian theologians. We should not allow accusations of anti-Semitism and Western guilt regarding the Holocaust to avert our eyes from Israel's colonial policies. Maybe the missionaries to the Americas in the sixteenth century were innocent, and maybe Brueggemann in the late 1970s was naïve, but it is time to end this theological innocence. We should confess that Christian theologians have played, consciously or subconsciously, a major role in aiding the ongoing colonization of Palestinian land and people. Land theology has been a theological tool for Palestinian dispossession and oppression. Christian theologians have failed to see that the promised land is confiscated land. The preoccupation of Christian theologians with the Bible, fear of being called anti-Semitic, and guilt about the Holocaust have disguised the ongoing colonization of Palestine. To these ends, the liberation of the Palestinian people and the liberation of theological minds are closely bound together.

[50]Steven Salaita, *Holy Land in Transit: Colonialism and the Quest for Canaan* (Syracuse, NY: Syracuse University Press, 2006), 179.

Toward a Decolonial Theology of the Land

An important element that has not been given enough attention in theological treatments of Palestine is the geopolitical situation, which requires examination of the context of the land and its native people. These two elements, land and people, are the most important hermeneutical keys to understanding and interpreting scripture.

Geopolitics and the Land

Historic Palestine is a territory located at the crossroads of three continents and has an image of being at the heart of the region, the "navel of the earth." This is myth, for, in reality, Palestine is a land on the margin, on the periphery of the Fertile Crescent, a border land for diverse empires. A close look at the map shows Palestine surrounded by five regional powers that have determined its fate: Egypt to the south, Europe to the west, Turkey to the north, and Mesopotamia and Persia to the northeast. Throughout history, Palestine has stood in the sphere of influence of one or two of these five powers, getting pulled in competing directions. Palestine's fertile plains have been the battleground for these conflicting powers, and it is hardly by chance that Armageddon is seen as taking place in the land's most fruitful valley.

Due to its geopolitical position, Palestine has been occupied or under the patronage of Egyptians, Assyrians, Babylonians, Persians, Greeks, Ptolemies, Seleucids, Romans, Byzantines, Arabs, Crusaders, Ottomans, British, and Israelis. While these superpowers were well established politically, having accumulated a culture of political dominance, the native peoples of Palestine were powerless most of the time, constantly adjusting their identity and boundaries within a changing context.

Adjustment, resistance, and liberation from occupation is a connecting thread of Palestine's history from the second millennium BC until today.

The land often came under more than one imperial power, fostering diverse identities. The influence of regional powers over Palestine created either a buffer zone or a battlefield where regional wars were fought. None could truly survive without the support of greater patrons. To look at these features of Palestine is to see how the geopolitics of the region determine the land's fate, a fate that is very difficult to escape. As a land under occupation, the theme of liberation was central throughout history as well as in the Bible. At the same time, control of the land and the unity of its peoples remains an uphill struggle. We cannot understand the land theology of the Bible outside of the geopolitical reality of Palestine, and we cannot understand the biblical message without analyzing the power structures of that time and today.

The Native People and the Land

Many Christian theologians and Zionist thinkers confuse the Israelites of the Bible with the Israelis of today. These theologians shift between 70 AD and 1948 as if history stood still for two millennia and as if the land of Palestine was "without a people" and waiting to be inhabited "again" by "a people without a land." The Israelis of today are not the direct descendants of the Israelites of the Bible, nor are the Palestinians of today the direct successors of the Philistines. Any such understanding is based on a static view of history and a fundamentalist approach to biblical literature.

Throughout history, most of Palestine's native people never left the land. Only a small minority of Palestine's people were deported. Empires came, occupied the land for a number of years or decades, but were eventually forced to leave. The majority of the native people remained in the land of their ancestors. They were the *am-ha'aretz*, the "people of the land," in spite of all the empires that controlled that land throughout its history. Identities did change in accordance with new realities and empires. People changed their language from Palestinian and Phoenician West Semitic to Aramaic and Hebrew, and later to Greek and Arabic. Their identity shifted from Canaanite to Philistine to Judahite and Israelite, to Hasmonaic, to Roman, to Byzantine, to Arab, to Ottoman and Palestinian, just to name a few. They changed religion from Ba'al to Yahweh. Later they believed in Jesus as Christ and became Christians, the first Aramaic-speaking Monophysites, before being forced to become, for example, Greek Orthodox. Obligated to pay extra taxes during Islamic dominance, they became Muslims. And yet, throughout the centuries, they maintained a dynamic and flexible identity. In this sense, Palestinians today stand in historic continuity with biblical Canaanites, Philistines, Israelites, and Judahites, and are the native people of the land. Irrespective of their religious affiliation (Muslims, Christians, Jews, and Samaritans), the Palestinian people demonstrate significant continuity from biblical times until the present, and they are the native people who survived empires and occupations. They comprise the remnants of invading armies or settlers who stayed and integrated themselves rather than returning to their original homeland. Palestinians are the outcome of this long and dynamic history. Their context is important for understanding the Bible. It is time to listen to the narrative of the native people of the land. Palestinian Jews belong to the people of the land, and followers of the Jewish faith have been part and parcel of the region throughout the last two millennia. But settler colonial Zionists are not part of the people of the land. They are invaders and subcontractors to the empires.

The Palestinians of today are the native people of the land because they are not part of the empire. Their voice is not only unheard but often silenced. Unless their discourse falls within a European framework, they are not considered dialogue partners. The Muslims of Palestine are ignored because they are Muslims and not thought of as part of the Judeo-Christian culture. Palestinian Christians are marginalized because they are Palestinians. And native, anti-Zionist Jews and Samaritans who are neither Zionist nor Ashkenazi are ignored as non-European. Many Western theologians want to monopolize the discourse and recognize only those Palestinians who use their frame of reference.

If we really want to understand the Bible's message, it is of the utmost importance to listen to Palestine's native people. Their suffering under occupation, their aspiration for liberation, their struggles and hopes are all relevant to exegesis. For the Palestinian people, land is life. It is ancestral heritage. They belong to this land and have nowhere else to go. They experience being made into aliens at home by Israeli policies. They see how Jewish immigrants occupy their land, build settlements, and obtain citizenship, while they, the native people, are marginalized and pushed out. Palestine is their homeland, but Palestinians in the diaspora are not allowed to enter the land of their fathers, whereas Jews are given the right to settle anywhere in Palestine irrespective of where they have come from. The land of Palestine is colonized by the use of military hardware that is justified by theological software. The natural right of Palestinians to the land of their ancestors is violated. This is not an exclusive Palestinian experience and is mirrored by many native peoples in North and South America, in Southern Africa, and in Australia. It is important to listen to the voice of these indigenous peoples. The Bible is the book that contains these voices, the voices of the colonized, not the colonizers.

Toward a Decolonial Reading of the Bible

The Bible contains books like Joshua that can be interpreted as a blueprint for settler colonialism. It also contains prophets who called for social justice. Like the bazaar in the Old City of Jerusalem, one can find many different ingredients in the Bible. There are texts that sanction colonization and texts that promote liberation. What we discover says more about us and what we are searching for as readers than about the Bible itself. For the remainder of the chapter, I offer a decolonial reading of two scriptural passages, one from the Old Testament and one from the New Testament, to demonstrate the hermeneutic of Palestinian liberation.

1 Kings 21

Ahab, King of Samaria, had a palace in Jezreel, but he was not satisfied with his large palace and coveted the vineyard of his neighbor Naboth. Ahab wanted Naboth's vineyard at any price. First, he offered Naboth a "better one," and he was also ready to pay with silver. The king acted in vain, for Naboth did not want to give away his ancestral inheritance because to keep it was something like a divine command for him. Ahab knew that, as King of Israel, he had no right to confiscate the land of an Israelite farmer; in accordance with Israelite faith, even the Israelite kings were subject to divine law. But Jezebel, the Sidonian king's daughter, thought differently and had a different understanding of royalty. She asked her husband whether he was really the King of Israel when he did nothing about Naboth's refusal. Jezebel's models were the imperial rulers who were absolute sovereigns. It was an occupier–occupied relationship where the law serves the empire and its policy of expansion.

Jezebel asked for two scoundrels to bear false witness against Naboth and claim he had cursed God and the king. The divinity of God and security of the state represented by the king were of utmost importance. Naboth was stoned to death, and Ahab was then free to confiscate all his possessions. In this context, the Prophet Elijah intervened because an injustice had been committed, God's commandments had been violated, and the court misused.

The story of Naboth is the story of thousands of Palestinians today whose lands are confiscated to enlarge the Jewish colonies in the West Bank that exploit the water and resources of the Palestinian people. Naboth's story is taking place almost on a daily basis in the West Bank. It is a clear violation of both divine law and international law, but very few theologians dare to raise a prophetic voice and term this land colonization by name.

Matthew 5:5

One of the sentences of Jesus that requires reinterpretation is Matthew 5:5: "Blessed are the meek for they will inherit the earth." This text is taken from the Sermon on the Mount according to Matthew. Compared with the other beatitudes of that sermon, this one is often neglected and seldom receives attention. The phrase "Blessed are the peacemakers" is cited frequently, but we rarely hear "Blessed are the meek for they will inherit the earth." Indeed, Luke skips this verse altogether. Interestingly, Luke likes to talk about the poor, the hungry, and the thirsty, but not about the meek!

This verse must have been largely ignored initially because it was translated incorrectly. Originally the verse was taken from Psalm 37, which does not refer to "the earth" but to "the land." In fact, "the land" is repeated several times in that psalm. It should, therefore, read, "Blessed are the meek; they will inherit the land." That perhaps makes better sense. Psalm 37 does not refer to land near and far but does speak about a certain land, Palestine. When Jesus said that the meek will inherit the land, everyone at the time knew what was meant by the land. He meant the Holy Land, Palestine. When the words of Jesus were translated from Aramaic into Greek, the word that means the land was changed to read the earth. In fact, in Arabic the word, *al-ard,* means both earth and land. Translation is interpretation, and earth replaced land.

The gospels were closely connected to a certain land, Palestine. For the early church located outside of Palestine, talking about the earth made far more sense. Why should somebody in Rome worry about who would inherit Palestine? They were concerned about their souls and maybe about their own land, but not about a distant one. Yet, one cannot understand the gospels if they are disconnected from their original context of Palestine.

I struggled with this text for many, many years. It simply did not make sense. I do not like to spiritualize things because I think Jesus always spoke about reality and refused to avoid it, which was the essence of his spirituality. For a long time, I thought that Jesus had been mistaken. One need only look around the West Bank to realize that 60 percent of it is controlled by the Israeli army and Jewish settlers. This glaring reality is one of the largest land thefts in modern history, worth hundreds of billions of dollars. The Israeli settlements that ring the West Bank make it obvious that the empire has inherited the land. Listening to the words of Jesus through Palestinian, Native American, Black South African, or Aboriginal Australian's ears does not make any more sense. He must have been mistaken! It is clear that the military occupation controls the land and its resources. Everything is controlled by the empire. The empire inherits the land, not the meek. Jesus was mistaken because the meek are crushed. Their land is being confiscated to make place for people brought in by the empire. Jesus was mistaken.

But over the last decade of struggling with this text, I have come to read it with new eyes. I discovered something more powerful than I expected. Matthew 5:5 actually speaks directly to reality in a way we would never imagine. It is necessary to use *longue durée* lenses because if the verse is read with regular lenses, we will never grasp its true meaning.[51] Our mistake has been to read history only with the current empire in mind. The prevailing empire has taken all of our attention. Only attending to the Israeli–Palestinian conflict from a perspective of the last sixty years, the words of Jesus do not make sense at all. But Jesus had wide-angle lenses and looked at history from a long-term perspective.

For people in the time of Jesus, the occupation began with the Romans. Jesus had a far greater understanding of the history of Palestine. He looked at a thousand years at once and saw a chain of empires. There is not a single regional empire that at some point did not occupy Palestine. The first was the Assyrian in 722 BC, which lasted for over two hundred years. The Assyrians were replaced by the Babylonians in 587, who were pushed out by the Persians in 538. The latter were forced to leave by Alexander the Great. Then there were the Romans. Two thousand years after Jesus, we can continue to recite the list of empires who ruled Palestine: the Byzantines; the Arabs; the Crusaders; the Ayyubids; the Ottomans; the British; and finally, the State of Israel. We have been trained to naively connect Israel today with the Israel of the Bible rather than with this chain of occupying empires. If we focus on the latter, the words of Jesus make perfect sense. None of those empires lasted in Palestine forever. They came and stayed for fifty, one hundred, two hundred, a maximum of four hundred years. Ultimately, they were all blown away, gone with the wind.

---

[51] *Longue durée* is an expression used by the French Annales School of historic writing that gives priority to long-term historical structures over events.

When occupied people face the empire, they are generally so overwhelmed by its power that they think that the empire will remain forever and has eternal power. Jesus wanted to tell his people that the empire would not last, that empires come and go. When empires collapse and depart, it is the poor and the meek who remain. Those people of the land who prosper emigrate and seek to grow richer within the centers of empire. Those who are well educated are claimed by the empire. Who remains on the land? The meek, that is, the powerless! Empires come and go, while the meek inherit the land. The wisdom of Jesus is staggering. It seems to me that we have been blinded by a theology that has failed to help us understand what Jesus was really saying.

Some might disagree, insisting that the Israeli occupation is different. They say, "Look at the settlements. How can you claim they will be gone one day? Look at the wall. How can you say it will be dismantled?" But Israel is no different from the empires of the past. The native people of Palestine who lived at the time of Jesus and saw the military checkpoints set up by Herod the Great, such as Herodian and Masada, could never have imagined that Herod and his empire would not be there permanently. To see the "settlements" built by Herod and his sons, such as Caesarea Maritima, Caesarea Philippi, Sepphoris, Tiberias, Sebastopol, Jerusalem, and others, it would have been almost inconceivable to question the durability of the Roman Empire. Jesus was telling the Palestinian Jews that the Romans who had built those colonies would not be there forever, and Palestine would be inherited by the meek. This is a direct critique of the settler colonial practice of the Romans. This is not a cheap hope in a distant future but a decolonial teaching. Jesus wanted to release the powerless from the power of the empire. The moment he spoke those words, the empire lost its power over the people, and power was transferred where it rightly belonged, with the people.

Conclusion

The land issue is not a mere theological topic but one of high political relevance. Historically, the notion of the promised land was used by Western Christian empires to colonize and exploit countries and continents. Today, no one would dare to evoke such a theology as a pretext for colonization, apart from the State of Israel. Over the past one hundred years, Israel has often used the Bible to justify the colonization of Palestinian land. The Zionist movement deliberately developed the ideology of "God, people, and land" as an inseparable unit, and this was adopted by conservative Christian Zionists, Christian Holocaust theologians, and other liberal Christian Zionists. While their adoption of this theology may have stemmed from formal anti-Judaic theologies or from guilt about the Holocaust, the result was that Israel was granted theological impunity to colonize Palestinian land. For Zionists and Christian Zionists, there is nothing wrong with settler colonialism. On the contrary, it is celebrated as the fulfillment of a divine land promise. This theology contradicts international law and is in violation of the Human Rights Charter. Yet, such theologies continue to be espoused by naïve or well-intended theologians, or others brought in by the Zionist movement.

It is high time to develop a theology that views the colonization of Palestine as part and parcel of European settler colonial history. Theologians should be troubled when the promised land becomes the colonized land, when indigenous people are robbed of their land and resources and left to be landless refugees or confined in reservations. During the last two decades, we have seen the emergence of new theological voices in Australia, Canada, and elsewhere recognizing the lawful owners of the land. Nothing like this has yet been seen in Israel. Theologians must listen to and amplify indigenous voices of the people of the land rather than being an uncensored echo of imperial colonial powers. For the current Israeli government to implement an ethno-nationalist policy of ethnic cleansing of the indigenous people based on an exclusive "biblical" myth-history should not be justified theologically or politically. Throughout history, Palestine has been pluralistic in nature. Until 1948, Christians, Jews, and Muslims shared the land and lived side by side. What is our vision for our land? Is our vision an exclusivist ethnocentric vision or an inclusive one that respects the plurality of peoples and their identities? This question is of utmost importance for the future of Palestine and also globally in a world facing ethno-national tensions, exclusive ideologies, and religious fanaticism.

In the context of land colonization, theologians must be very careful not to supply the colonizer with the ideological tools to support their oppression.

What can hermeneutics, as we have been studying it, contribute to the *ethical* dilemmas posed when texts of power become texts of terror? Can we stand neutral as mere "academic interpreters"? Is hermeneutics necessarily a political activity? We need to be aware that the pernicious political policy of apartheid in South Africa had its beginnings in specific biblical hermeneutics that saw all things created as distinct under God, their differences to be clearly acknowledged.[52]

We might also recall that apartheid in South Africa arose, to some extent at least, from biblical criticism and interpretation. In the postcolonial era of the present day it is easy to see how a very difficult hermeneutic pertains, and how not only is the Bible to be read in different ways in the light of political and social experience, but the power of the new reader must

---

[52]David Jasper, *A Short Introduction to Hermeneutics* (Louisville, KY: Westminster John Knox Press, 2004), 123–24.

be turned against old prejudices that were once regarded as unquestioned truths.[53]

We cannot separate Israeli colonial policies in Palestine from modern European colonial history. No credible theologian today would accept a land theology from the Whites that justifies settler colonialism in South Africa, North America, or Australia. Why would they accept it from Israel? Why is Israel's colonization of Palestine seen as unique, biblical, and different from all others? We cannot be so theologically naïve to talk about "the land," meaning Palestine, without reflecting on the current use of land ideology by Jewish colonial settlers. No one should be allowed, whether Jewish settlers, Israeli politicians, or naïve Christian theologians, to use "biblical rights" to violate "human rights." We should not allow accusations of anti-Semitism and Western guilt about the Holocaust to avert our eyes from Israel's colonial policies. Maybe missionaries to the Americas in the 1sixteenth century were innocent, and Brueggemann in the late 1970s may have been naïve, but now is the time to end this theological innocence. We ought to confess that Christian theologians have played a key role, consciously or subconsciously, in aiding the ongoing colonization of Palestinian land and people. A decolonial theology of the land is urgently required.

---

[53]Ibid., 125.

4

Chosen People?

The issue of chosenness is much more problematic than people or even theologians might think, and on so many levels: theological, philosophical, and political. Theologically speaking, election is not one specific and isolated theological *topos*. It poses the fundamental question of biblical hermeneutics: how to understand the biblical story and how to translate it into our period of time. Election does not stand alone but is connected to theological topics such as chosen people, covenant, and promised land, and it is embedded within larger Christian–Jewish relations. What hermeneutical key is appropriate today for Christians when dealing with an ancient text, especially that of the Old Testament? Who is elected: individuals, a group of people, a nation? "Israel"? How do we define "Israel"? A race? A religion? A state? The church?

In this book, we make a point to distinguish between four different usages of the word *Israel*. Biblically and historically speaking, the name *Israel* refers in the Bible mainly to the northern part of Palestine during a relatively short period of time known as the Kingdom of Israel or House of Omri (tenth century to 722 BCE). This political entity must be distinguished from biblical Israel as an abstract theological concept to describe "God's people." Both are different from "Ancient

Israel" as a modern construct that confuses certain aspects of the biblical story with history, thereby projecting an exclusive ethno-national and religious state into the Bible.[1] Then there is a modern political entity called the State of Israel. These four different "Israels" are not interchangeable and have to be distinguished from each other, from Judaism, and people of Jewish faith. At the same time, it is important to distinguish between the Judeans of the Bible, meaning the people who were living in the southern part of Palestine, and the Jews of today, on the one hand, and between the Israelites of the Bible and Israelis today, on the other. Any confusion leads to theological misconceptions and political misjudgments. Meanwhile, Palestine does not refer to a political, religious, or ethnic entity but to a multiethnic, multicultural, and multireligious region that was able to include diverse identities and peoples within its boundaries. When using the term *people of the land* or the *people of Palestine*, I refer to this inclusive nature of the people who resided on it irrespective of their religious, ethnic, or national identity. This inclusive nature of Palestine and its people remained until 1948, when the name Palestine was replaced with Israel.

Confusion was triggered after 1948, when persecuted European Jews established a state in Palestine and chose the name Israel for it. This confusion became more obvious after the 1967 war. For centuries prior, mainstream Christian theology propagated that the Jews, previously elected by God, were rejected because they did not accept Christ as their Messiah and that the Christians are now the new elected ones and God's chosen people. This supremacist Christian "rejection theology" was the theological undercurrent of the social discrimination experienced by Jews in Europe that culminated in the Holocaust. This tragic history, coupled with a concentrated effort by Jewish

---

[1] Keith W. Whitelam, *The Invention of Ancient Israel: The Silencing of Palestinian History* (London: Routledge, 1996).

theologians against *supersessionism,* known also as *replacement theology* (meaning that the church has replaced Israel), pushed many Christian theologians to rethink their traditional approach to the notion of election.

While they could not give up the notion that Christians are the elected people, Christian theologians in the 1950s started opening up their theological tent to include the Jews, stating that God's promises in the Old Testament remain valid for modern-day Jews. In the United States, this development followed closely after the political classification of Jews as White in the G.I. Bill (along with Irish and Italian Catholics) under the Roosevelt administration.[2] It is no surprise that Western theological revision and racial upgrading went hand in hand. While challenging the traditional Christian *replacement theology,* Christians unintentionally created a theology that, politically speaking, replaced Palestinians, the indigenous people of the land, with European Jews. Palestinian rights to a life in freedom and dignity on their native land was the sacrifice offered by European theologians as restitution for Christian anti-Judaism and the Holocaust.

While churches in the West moved to include Jews in their theology, Muslims were excluded. But if followers of the three monotheistic religions believe that God has elected them, how can we deal with multiple claims of election by Jews, Christians, and Muslims? The seventeenth-century Jewish philosopher Baruch Spinoza complicates the question, asking, does it make sense for God to divinely elect a particular group of people?[3] Can we, who live in a post-Enlightenment era of human rights and fundamental equality between people, believe in a God

---

[2]For details, see Karen Brodkin, *How Jews Became White Folks and What That Says About Race in America* (New Brunswick, NJ: Rutgers University Press, 1998).

[3]David Novak, *The Election of Israel: The Idea of the Chosen People,* reissue ed. (Cambridge: Cambridge University Press, 2007), 22–49.

who discriminates between people, with some being elected, and others not elected or even some elected to be damned (Genesis 6:8; 9:18–27; Deuteronomy 7:2)? Furthermore, how, then, are we to justify God's command of genocide against the unelected, like the Canaanites and the other people of the land (Deuteronomy 7)?[4]

Additionally, we must address the context in modern history in which the notion of an elected and chosen people was developed and utilized. What was and is the *Sitz im Leben* for divine election in modern Western nationalism? What reception history lies behind it? Is there a responsible way to talk about election today, or is it better to leave it behind? There is no way to deal with all of these difficult questions in this particular chapter, but I will try my best to tackle the most pressing questions that arise from within the Palestinian context.

Election as a Challenge for Palestinian Christians

As if these questions were not complicated enough for the Palestinian people in general, and Palestinian Christians in particular, they constitute theological and theoretical challenges and, significantly, an existential threat. Many Palestinian Christians struggle with the question of how to understand the issue of election in the Old Testament, which constitutes an integral part of the biblical canon. Palestinian Christians feel that their existence is threatened when the Hebrew Bible is interpreted as the history of Jews as people and when the notion of election is weaponized politically to give modern Israelis a *carte blanche* for their discriminatory policies. Palestinian Christians feel threatened when election is connected to the notion of a

---

[4]See, as an example, Stanley N. Gundry et al., *Show Them No Mercy: 4 Views on God and Canaanite Genocide* (Grand Rapids: Zondervan Academic, 2003).

promised land as a theological pretext to occupy their Palestinian homeland. For Palestinians who have lived under several forms of Israeli occupation for over seven decades, the Bible has often been used to legitimize the occupation of Palestinian land and people. Israel does not occupy the land of Palestine purely with the military *hardware* (hard power) provided by the United States and several European countries, but the State of Israel, Zionist Jews, and their many Christian Zionist allies weaponize the Bible to provide the occupation with the needed *software*, that is, soft power. Divine election is an integral part of this software.

The military occupation of Palestinian land and people is blurred with biblical concepts like "God's chosen people" and "land promise." Political and military injustice are covered up by a theological language that equates biblical Israel with the State of Israel today. In this context, the State of Israel is not judged in the same way as any other state, but rather as a theopolitical reality, as a state with theological qualities, and the Israelis are judged as people with a unique divine destiny. This results in a political bias toward the State of Israel that bears important military ramifications. In the Palestinian–Israeli context, "divine rights" are often used to legitimize the violent violation of Palestinian human rights.

Conversely, within this apparently "biblical logic," Palestinians are equated either with the Philistines of the Bible, as the enemies of "Israel," or as the nonelect, as cursed Canaanites. As Arabs and Arab Christians, Palestinians are seen as the descendants of Ishmael, meaning people with a lesser theological status than the descendants of Isaac, who are represented by the Israelis of today. As Arabs, Palestinians are equated with Muslims, resulting in Christians preferring Jews over and against Muslims. This choice blends with the Islamophobia of the post-9/11 era and further complicates the already complex. These racist connections are widespread among Jews and Christians, often present in subconscious bias if not explicitly expressed in social and political life. Biblical interpretation of election provides the blueprint for racial and ethnic discrimination. While some Christians might sympathize with the humanitarian situation of Palestinians, their emotional and theological bond remains with the Israelis because they are seen as God's elected people with a unique entitlement.

Despite the importance of this topic, no Palestinian theologian to date has published a monograph or scholarly piece explicitly discussing the notion of *election* or *chosen people* in the Bible. Before presenting my own theological understanding of election in this chapter, I briefly present three different Palestinian theological perspectives that have dealt with the issue to some degree. Palestinian theology is diverse, and differences do not necessarily run along denominational lines. I have chosen three prominent Palestinian figures from three different Christian denominations: the Anglican theologian Naim Ateek, representing mainline Protestant theology; Father Paul Tarazi, a Greek Orthodox theologian; and the Latin Patriarch Michel Sabbah. Ateek and Sabbah wrote first and foremost in their pastoral capacity, while Tarazi wrote as a scholar teaching biblical theology. Sabbah's pastoral letter was a collective effort by several priests and theologians of the diocese.

Naim Ateek

Naim Ateek was born in the Palestinian city of Bisan in 1937. In 1948, during the *Nakba*, his village was destroyed by Israeli forces, forcing his family to leave and to seek refuge in Nazareth. Ateek completed all of his theological studies in the United States and was ordained as an Anglican priest in 1967. In 1989, during the first Palestinian uprising known as the Intifada, Ateek established Sabeel, the ecumenical liberation theology center. In that same year, he published his book *Justice and Only Justice: A*

Palestinian Theology of Liberation.[5] This was a first attempt by a Palestinian Christian to articulate a theology of liberation for the Palestinian context. Although Ateek does not address the issue of election explicitly in this book, the hermeneutics presented shed enough light to extract his understanding of the subject. As a pastor of a Palestinian Anglican parish, Ateek struggled in the context of the Intifada to find a hermeneutic that would allow his parishioners "to identify the authentic Word of *God* in the Bible, and to discern the true meaning of those biblical texts that Jewish Zionists and Christian fundamentalists cite to substantiate their subjective claims and prejudices."[6]

For Ateek, the hermeneutical key is "nothing less than Jesus Christ himself. For in Christ, through Christ, and because of Christ, Christians have been given a revealed insight into God's nature and character."[7] Based on these criteria, Ateek distinguishes between three different strata in the Old Testament that represent different stages in human understanding of God: the nationalist, the Torah oriented, and the prophetic. He found the nationalist stream in the books of Joshua, Judges, Samuel, and Kings, best represented later by the zealots. "These books are characterized by their favorable reporting of the use of force to achieve the Israelites' national goals. The later proponents of this tradition believed that the Jews had a special, privileged relationship with God."[8] He found the Torah-oriented stream in the first five books of the Bible, best represented later by the Pharisees and Rabbinic Judaism. The third stream is the prophetic, which possesses a "deep, profound, and mature understanding of God."[9] The Prophets "were able to produce

---

[5]Naim Stifan Ateek, *Justice and Only Justice: A Palestinian Theology of Liberation* (Maryknoll, NY: Orbis Books, 1989).
[6]Ibid., 79.
[7]Ibid., 79–80.
[8]Ibid., 94.
[9]Ibid., 96.

profound truths about the universal and inclusive nature of God, although these insights are set within a massive quantity of material that is narrow, nationalist, and exclusive."[10] For Ateek, Jesus clearly stood in this prophetic tradition and represented its clearest form amid the prevailing nationalistic and legalistic concepts of his time. The core value of the prophetic tradition is justice, which explains the title of his first book *Justice and Only Justice,* and a later book *A Palestinian Theology of Liberation: The Bible, Justice and the Palestine-Israel Conflict.*[11]

Based on this hermeneutic, Ateek understands election as a symptom of the nationalistic stream and a tribal understanding of God. This tribal understanding of God is already questioned in the Old Testament by prophets like Jonah, Amos, and Isaiah. Thus, the Bible is clear and moves from the particular to the universal, from the election of one nation to the calling of one people from all nations through Christ. For Ateek, this movement found its climax in Jesus; as Christians we cannot afford to revert to a tribal or nationalistic notion of God or God's people.

Paul Nadim Tarazi

Paul Tarazi's family was originally from Gaza. Paul was born in Jaffa. In 1948, his family was displaced and found refuge in Egypt before moving to Lebanon. Paul completed all of his theological studies at the Orthodox Theological Institute in Bucharest, Romania. In 1975, he migrated to the United States where he was ordained as a priest and served two Orthodox congregations, later teaching at St. Vladimir's Orthodox Theological Seminary in Crestwood, New York. There is no way to examine all the writings of Paul Tarazi regarding his understanding and

---

[10]Ibid.

[11]Naim Stifan Ateek, *A Palestinian Theology of Liberation: The Bible, Justice, and the Palestine-Israel Conflict* (Maryknoll, NY: Orbis Books, 2017).

handling of the *election theme*. His biblical commentaries and introductory volumes are too many to cover.[12] Rather, I will focus here on two publications: *Land and Covenant* published in 2009, and his article "Hermeneutical Shifts vis-à-vis Palestine in the Twentieth Century: Romans 9–11."[13] Neither of these pieces tackles the notion of election directly, but they discuss hermeneutics in general and covenant in relation to land in particular.

Tarazi's hermeneutical key is different than that of Ateek. For Tarazi, it is important to realize that the Bible, which Tarazi keeps referring to as the biblical story, has a clear beginning and a clear end. It ends with "Jesus's teaching being carried out to all nations until the end of age." As such, the biblical story is complete and closed. It does not have a sequel, nor does it allow for a history of a people to be continued beyond the limits of the scriptural canon.

> To consider that it does is sheer blasphemy since the assumption would be that there is still something of value for the human beings besides or over and above the teaching Word of God in the Old Testament and the teaching Word of Jesus in the New Testament. The fact that the biblical story is complete and closed as the Word of God and the Word of his ultimate messenger is reflected in that it forms a "canon," which is a Greek term (kanon) meaning "rule" or "ruler," that is, an authoritative reference.[14]

---

[12]A complete list of Tarazi's publications is found on his website: https://www.paul-nadim-tarazi.org/publications.html.

[13]Paul Nadim Tarazi, *Land and Covenant* (St. Paul, MN: OCABS Press, 2009); Paul Nadim Tarazi, "Hermeneutical Shifts vis-à-vis Palestine in the Twentieth Century: Romans 9–11," in *The Invention of History: A Century of Interplay between Theology and Politics in Palestine*, ed. Mitri Raheb (Bethlehem: Diyar, 2011), 167–84.

[14]Tarazi, *Land and Covenant*, 241.

Unlike Ateek, Tarazi does not distinguish between different streams within the Bible. For him, the biblical story is not a human story or history but is first and foremost the story of God, and the "only 'history' they contain is a repeat of the biblical story."[15] To clarify this point, Tarazi refers to three features of the Bible. First, "the traditional nomenclature of the biblical books and sections do not reflect an interest in human history." Rather, the titles of the three main parts of the Old Testament—Law, Prophets, and Wisdom—reflect an interest in the teaching.[16] Second, the biblical authors themselves were not interested in any historical events except to show that the Kings of Israel and Judah were unfaithful to God's law. Other historical aspects of the monarchs are dismissed with the stereotypical formula that they are "written in the Book of the Chronicles." In the Bible, the glorious deeds were not performed by the people themselves or by their heroes but by God himself, which makes the whole Bible nothing but God's story and law. For Tarazi, it is very clear "that the Bible is neither a book describing the history of a given people nor one containing the decipherment of future events. It is intended to be an instruction, a lesson."[17]

With this hermeneutic in mind, Tarazi addresses Romans 9–11. There, he dismisses the thesis of two independent paths to salvation. "God's olive tree is one and its branches are the one progeny of Abraham as defined in 4:13–25."[18] The two covenants theory is an expression of a "dispensationalist aberration" that was triggered, according to Tarazi, prior to 1948 by Karl Barth, who was influenced in his "church and Israel" theology by the German dispensationalist theologian Stroeter. Barth injected this dispensationalism into post–World War I

---

[15]Ibid., 249.

[16]Ibid., 253.

[17]Ibid., 265.

[18]Tarazi, "Hermeneutical Shifts vis-à-vis Palestine in the Twentieth Century: Romans 9–11," 169.

theology, and, through students like Paul van Buren and Jürgen Moltmann, Barth was able to influence a whole generation of post-Holocaust Christian theologians.[19]

Tarazi is critical of such dispensationalism that granted the Jews a theological status. Based on his hermeneutic, the resulting theological status of election is not canonical but was read into the text itself by later theologians. "How can something still be a canon, a rule by which everything else is to be assessed and judged, while it is subjected to our consistently shifting understanding or, to use a technical term, to its Wirkungsgeschichte?"[20] Tarazi refers here to his idea of the biblical story being complete and closed. To clarify this further, Tarazi gives an example from the New Testament.

> All the Pauline letters are addressed to localized communities, even when the same letter is addressed at the same time to many churches (Gal 1:2). This means that any other church, even when within the same province, is only secondarily addressed . . . However, this does not give license to the 21st century Corinthians or Thessalonians to assume that they are in a more privileged position than the rest of us. The reason is evident: the community Paul addressed is bound not only in space (area), *but also in time* . . . The same principle applies to the Old Testament scripture.[21]

For Tarazi, the main hermeneutical problem is that many Christian and Jewish theologians assume that they are *as such* the "church" or the "people of God," thus projecting the textual context into their own time and space. Such an understanding

---

[19]Ibid., 171.
[20]Ibid., 177.
[21]Ibid., 178.

led European Christians in the Middle Ages to consider Jerusalem *their city*, thus waging the Crusades.

It is on the same basis that 20th century Jews considered Palestine, and even greater Syria, as *theirs* and, as a corollary, considered any non-Jew living there as a Canaanite to be exterminated or removed through a form of apartheid. For one who claims to believe in scripture as a canon, such extrapolation is sheer blasphemy against the scriptural God who did what he did and said what he said one and for all times within the special and temporal limits of the already closed canon.[22]

For Tarazi, all realities within scripture are "exclusively scriptural realities, including God and Israel"[23] and are nothing but a challenging message, a *masal*. Any attempt to project it beyond the spatial and temporal limits of scripture would leave the scripture at the "mercy of the highest or most cunning bidder."[24] For Tarazi, it is clear that the Palestinians are the ones asked to pay the price of such a theology. Based on this understanding, Tarazi rejects any exegesis that reads Romans 9–11 or election "as a 'mystical' prediction of the fate of the Jews in the 20th and 21st centuries."[25] Such a reading would make Paul a fortune teller and not an apostle.

Patriarch Michel Sabbah

Michel Sabbah was born in Nazareth in 1933. He did his priestly studies at the Latin Patriarchal Seminary in Beit Jala and

---

[22]Ibid., 178–79.
[23]Ibid., 181.
[24]Ibid., 184.
[25]Ibid., 180.

was ordained as a priest in 1955. His PhD was completed at the Sorbonne in Arabic language. In 1988, he became the first native and non-Italian Latin Patriarch in Jerusalem. Patriarch Sabbah was one of the authors of the Kairos Palestine Document.[26] In 1993, two months after the signing of the Oslo Accords between Israel and the Palestine Liberation Organization, Patriarch Sabbah published his fourth pastoral letter, entitled "Reading the Bible Today in the Land of the Bible."[27] Sabbah wrote this letter to his priests, nuns, and parishioners, mainly Arab Palestinians and Jordanians, who had lived through the political conflict and experienced anguish and doubts when confronted with the Bible.[28] "Reading the Bible, the Word of God, is a difficult, sensitive and delicate task," he wrote, "since the matters to be tackled are related to our daily life. They even concern our very national and personal identity as believers, because unilateral, partial interpretations run the risk for some people of bringing into question their presence and permanence in this land which is their homeland."[29]

The pastoral letter aimed to address three questions. The first related to the relationship between the Old and the New Testament. The second related to the violence that is attributed to God in the Bible and how it is to be understood. The third was, "What influence do the promises, the gift of the land, the election and the covenant have for relations between Palestinians and Israelis? Is it possible for a just and merciful God to impose injustice or oppression on another people in order to favor the people He has chosen?"[30] Before answering these questions, the

[26]"Kairos Palestine: A Moment of Truth. A Word of Faith, Hope and Love from the Heart of Palestinian Suffering" (Bethlehem: Diyar, 2009).

[27]"Fourth Pastoral Letter of Patriarch Sabbah, November 1993," Latin Patriarchate of Jerusalem, https://www.lpj.org/website-archives/fourth-pastoral-letter-patriarch-sabbah-reading-bible-today-land-bible-november-1993-5e45d3114195b.

[28]Ibid., 2.

[29]Ibid., 3.

[30]Ibid., 8.

letter discussed the nature of the Word of God and presented
its hermeneutics. The letter made clear from the beginning
that the whole Bible, the Old as well as the New Testament, is
God's Word. Yet, it is a divine work through human deeds and
words.[31] To fully understand the Word of God, and in a good
Catholic fashion, faith within the community is a prerequisite:
"Today, we can develop a true understanding of Scripture only
in communion with the Church, in the light of Tradition, and
through the living liturgy and progress in Biblical studies."[32]

The document goes on to present what it calls a "progressive revelation," meaning that "the truth concerning God and
the message of salvation was not communicated only at one
time, once and for all. God adapted Himself to the history of
humankind and its ability to understand His revealed Word."[33]
This progression becomes visible through the different covenants
expressed by God through human history, starting with the
covenant with Noah involving the whole of creation; then the
covenant with Abraham, the father of Jews, Christians, and
Muslims; followed by the Sinai Covenant with Moses through
the law; to the covenant with David combining the royal throne
and temple; and ending with the new covenant of Jesus and the
establishment of the church as the new people of God.[34] The
letter makes it very clear that Jesus is the hermeneutical key to
reading the scripture. In a dialectical way, Jesus fulfilled this
while at the same time critiquing all three parts of the Old Testament: Law, Prophets, and the Wisdom Writings. Thus, Jesus
represents both the continuity of God's history of salvation and
a discontinuity by introducing a new covenant.[35]

Following this extensive hermeneutical discourse, the final

---

[31]Ibid., 10–12.
[32]Ibid., 14.
[33]Ibid.
[34]Ibid., 16–22.
[35]Ibid., 25–32.

section of the pastoral letter translates its hermeneutics to the question of election, covenant, promises, and the gift of land. This section discusses the political dimension of the existential question. Since the letter was published in November 1993, two months after the signing of the Oslo Accords at the White House, it avoids talking about the occupation and deploys an optimistic tone as if a new political era with hope for genuine peace were around the corner. It reiterates that the Bible is concerned first and foremost with the salvation of humanity. The letter explicitly asks the question that is on the mind of many Palestinians: Why the election of a people? It is interesting that the letter avoids calling people by name such as the Jewish people. This may have been a deliberate move to avoid confusing the people of the Bible with modern-day Israelis. It is also interesting that the letter quotes the Quran, talking about God choosing the *Children of Israel "Bani Israil."*[36] It is as if the Patriarch wants to assure his parishioners that the idea of election of a people is not only biblical but also Quranic.

The letter answers the question "why choose a people" by stressing that God chose a particular people to prepare the way for the coming of the Savior of the whole world: "In Scripture, God chose the Jewish people through whom He would call all the peoples of the earth to faith in God and in the Messiah whom He would send as the Saviour of the world."[37] This corresponds with the notion of a progressive revelation explained earlier. The letter proceeds to explain that election is, therefore, "a gratuitous act of love on God's part." It has nothing to do with any merit on the part of the people and requires from the chosen people a responsibility before God and humankind. Suddenly in this section and without any introduction, the letter moves on to speak in a pastoral tone about the election of individuals: "Every

---

[36]Ibid., 48.
[37]Ibid.

person is the object of God's choice and Love,"[38] while in other sections, it seems to address the two national or three religious groups living in the Holy Land: "It is in the humility lived by both, and in their common vision of God's action, that they will come together in love, justice and finally to reconciliation."[39]

The letter then discusses the issue of covenant and land, demonstrating the idea of "progressive revelation" as the guiding principle from the time of Abraham, who wandered through the land, to the time of Joshua with an armed conquest, to the careful administration of the land according to the law. The prophets warned of losing the land and being exiled because of idolatry, and, while in exile, they spoke of a new beginning with a new covenant and a new people. Yet, throughout salvation history, it was clear that the land belongs to God and the people are guests. In the New Testament, the land is then transformed and spiritualized. Heavenly Jerusalem replaces earthly Jerusalem.

> The concept of the land had then evolved throughout different stages of Revelation, beginning with the physical, geographical, and political concept, and ending with the spiritual and symbolic meaning. The worship of God is no longer linked to a specific land. A specific land is not the prime and absolute value for worship. The sole and absolute value is God and the worship of God in any place in the world.[40]

In the concluding part of the document, Sabbah tackles the real dilemma facing the people living on the land today. On the one hand, there are Jews who understand themselves as a people connected to the Old Testament and who found refuge in Palestine from the European pogroms. On the other hand, the

---

[38]Ibid.
[39]Ibid., 49.
[40]Ibid., 52.

Palestinians also understand themselves as a people and have been living on the land for centuries. On top of those national realities, there are people of three faiths, Jews, Christians, and Muslims, for whom the land is holy. Two peoples claim political rights, and three religions claim religious rights. For Sabbah, the distinction between political rights and religious rights is important.

Religious rights do not constitute political rights. Political rights and claims have to adhere to international law. Religion can provide moral and human values that can help guide politicians. Yet, the pastoral letter is aware that religions were often part of the problem.

> In certain periods of the history of salvation, political or military action was directly attributed to God. God was the God of armies. He fought with His faithful to defeat the pagans. God was immanent in history from an anthropomorphical and national perspective. Today humankind is better able to perceive God's transcendence. The word of faith is able to raise God above human conflicts in order to see Him as He is: a God who has chosen a people, but who is at the same time Father of all His human creatures, and no longer a God of war, a friend of one people, and fighting against another people.[41]

In this sense, Sabbah pleads to free the Bible from political manipulation and to see it as the Word of God in an invitation for people of faith to seek justice and reconciliation.

Election in the Modern Context

In a traditional theological approach, one would stop here in the belief that analysis of the biblical passages and their

[41]Ibid., 54.

application of the findings in the modern context is sufficient. Yet, there is no way to write about election without looking at its *Wirkungsgeschichte* (reception history) and its utilization in modern history. In this context, it is imperative to briefly mention three recent manifestations of the notion of election in the political sphere: nationalism and Zionism, settler colonialism, and American exceptionalism. All three have had a global impact on international politics and a direct impact on the Palestinian issue.

Nationalism

Election returned to theological prominence with the blending of religion and nationalism at the height of nineteenth-century imperialism. In a comparative study conducted at Harvard Divinity School in 1991 on *Divine Election and Western Nationalism,* several scholars examined the notion of chosen people in Protestant Europe and the United States between 1870 and 1914, arriving at the following conclusion:

> Nothing inspired this symbiosis of nationalism and Christianity more than the chosen people model as it derived, accurately or not, from the Hebrew scriptures. Indeed, without such symbols as the "Old Testament" account of a chosen people, a people united under God, the frequently powerful union of nationalism and Christianity might well have been less feasible in nations like Great Britain, Germany, or the United States. This biblical narrative . . . provided a mythical structure capable of defining the goals and aspirations of a nation.[42]

---

[42]William R. Hutchison, *Many Are Chosen: Divine Election and Western Nationalism,* ed. Hartmut Lehmann (Minneapolis: Fortress Press, 1994), 288.

The Harvard study clearly showed how chosen people ideologies were an important element of imperial policies in Germany after 1870, Great Britain, and the United States. "In these cases, to differing degrees, the claim of chosenness was made part of both the domestic and the foreign policy outlined by the ruling groups. In such cases the chosen people *topos* served as a means of legitimation for domination and as a tool of suppression for those who did not conform."[43] The idea of chosen people was utilized within the national discourse to combat the modernization, de-Christianization, and secularization of Europe by creating an alliance between Christianity and nationalism.[44] In this context, the nation-state was projected into the Bible, and biblical Israel became the prototype of the chosen nation. It should be no wonder that, during this time, Christian Zionism experienced a revival with a zeal to revive "ancient Israel" in Palestine.

Influenced by both European nationalism and Christian Zionism, Jewish Zionism emerged in Europe as one of the answers to the Jewish dilemma of persecution, conversion, or assimilation. Following the ideals of romantic nationalism, European Jews in pursuit of normalcy wanted to be a "nation like all other nations," with an ideal land (Palestine), (socialist) state, special language (Hebrew), identifiable national customs, and a unique mission to "once again become the chosen of the peoples!!"[45] Martin Buber warned of blindly copying European nationalism while abandoning election as a religious task, for doing so would mean nothing less than "national assimilation."[46]

---

[43]Ibid., 292.
[44]Ibid., 287.
[45]Paul Mendes-Flohr, "In Pursuit of Normalcy: Zionism's Ambivalence toward Israel's Election," in *Many Are Chosen: Divine Election and Western Nationalism*, ed. William R. Hutchison and Hartmut Lehmann (Minneapolis: Augsburg Fortress, 1994), 220.
[46]Ibid., 224.

It is important here to mention that not all Jews have embraced Zionism. In 1885, the Pittsburgh conference of the American reform movement declared, "We consider ourselves no longer a nation, but a religious community, and therefore expect neither a return to Palestine, nor a sacrificial worship under the administration of the sons of Aaron, nor the restoration of any of the laws concerning the Jewish state."[47] Unfortunately, a third stream in European Judaism got the upper hand and developed to be the best organized in today's State of Israel. These are the Jews who pursue a settler colonial policy against the Palestinian people and land. However, it is important to consider this broad spectrum of Judaism, from anti-Zionist Judaism to settler colonial Judaism, and the different ways Jews have been interpreting election over time.[48]

Settler Colonialism

The belief in a kind of *divine election* and mission has been an important feature of settler colonialism in different regions and at different periods, from the Spanish and Portuguese colonization and settlement of Latin America, to White settlement in southern Africa, and the Zionist conquest and settlement in Palestine.[49] In his book *God's Peoples: Covenant and Land in South Africa, Israel, and Ulster*, Akenson looked at Ulster Presbyterians of Northern Ireland, Afrikaners of South Africa, and Jews in Israel.[50] What the three groups have in common is a "covenantal mind-set." These settler colonial groups view

---

[47]Todd Gitlin and Liel Leibovitz, *The Chosen Peoples: America, Israel, and the Ordeals of Divine Election*, reprint ed. (New York: Simon & Schuster, 2013), 30.

[48]For more details, see S. Leyla Gurkan, *The Jews as a Chosen People: Tradition and Transformation* (London: Routledge, 2008).

[49]Michael Prior, *The Bible and Colonialism: A Moral Critique* (Sheffield, UK: Sheffield Academic Press, 1997), 11.

[50]Donald Harman Akenson, *God's Peoples: Covenant and Land in South Africa, Israel, and Ulster* (Ithaca, NY: NCROL, 1992).

themselves as a chosen people with a sacred claim to a promised land. They cultivate a devotion to a warrior god, a belief in a threat of an external enemy, and an exodus experience. While some countries like Canada and Australia are trying to confront their country's history of settler colonialism, the State of Israel is proudly and unapologetically pushing their settler colonial project with full power by de facto annexing Palestinian land while excluding the Palestine native people.

American Exceptionalism

The notion of election has played a prominent role in American culture over the past five decades. The 1967 war gave a boost to American Christian Zionism. As mentioned in an earlier chapter, the fact that the United States lost the war in Vietnam while Israel won against several Arab states was seen both as proof of Israel's divine election and as a sign of American jeremiad.[51] The notion of election is often translated into American culture as American exceptionalism. The American Christian Right views

America as the New Israel, or less directly, as a divinely elect nation of the contemporary world chosen to save the world via its politics, economics, and culture as well as its own innate moral goodness, if only it stays true to its true self. These narratives interweave elements of the biblical narrative with those of American history and myth, resulting in a syncretized nationalist narrative of American chosenness that equates faithfulness to America with faithfulness to Jesus Christ, thus making American national identity a gospel imperative.[52]

---

[51]Andrew R. Murphy, *Prodigal Nation: Moral Decline and Divine Punishment from New England to 9/11* (Oxford: Oxford University Press, 2008).
[52]Braden P. Anderson, *Chosen Nation* (Eugene, OR: Cascade Books, 2012),

The bond between the State of Israel and the United States is of a strategic political and military nature, and is grounded in a common belief of being a chosen people as a settler community called to rule. In today's context, election is often expressed as White supremacy and as a Jewish (Ashkenazi) supremacy with racist undertones. Such ideology has had a profound and dangerous international influence on American policy on Palestine and the larger Arab world. The domestic danger of this theology was evident in the act of insurrection on the US Capitol in January 2021, incited by President Trump, when members of the American religious right, including many Christian Zionists, stormed the Capitol, leading to the deaths of five people.

Toward a New Decolonial Understanding of Election

The three theological perspectives presented here are important and helpful in their own ways. However, there is an important element missing in them. While all three authors struggle with the current realities triggered by having a state with a biblical name, "Israel," they read the Bible through a purely Christian biblical lens that does not give enough attention to the sociopolitical context of the Bible itself. The perspectives tend, therefore, to be dogmatic in nature that would make sense only to Christians. In this section, I will present a decolonial perspective of the notion of election that I have developed in my work as a Palestinian theologian in the early twenty-first century.

Story or History

A fundamental question in biblical hermeneutics is how to view the Bible. Is it a story or history? Biblical hermeneutics that

---

250–51.

prioritize the Bible as a book of history, whether the history of a certain people or the history of God, are a critical characteristic of religious fundamentalism and have no place in a decolonial theological approach to the theme of election. The Bible is a story, not necessarily God's own story but the story of people with God. It is the story of certain groups of people at certain times over one millennium, with certain cultural backgrounds, including Semitic and Greek, in a certain geographic radius, including Palestine and the Middle East, with God. God's own story is bigger, richer, and more difficult to grasp.

God's own story cannot be confined to such a short period of the universe's history or reduced to one region, or, as a matter of fact, to one planet. God's story is not the exclusive story of people with God. As Christians, we do not believe that the Bible simply descended from heaven to us. It is the Word, Christ, that descended to us from heaven, not words (John 3:13). The words were written by people like us, written in certain sociocultural, religious, and political contexts, and with specific aims. Those writers were inspired to write this story with God.

Jews, Christians, and Muslims continue to relate to and feel inspired by this particular story that we know as the Bible. The story is not self-explanatory and needs to be retold and reinterpreted. To keep the story relevant, the monotheistic religions have had to keep translating the story for each generation and for each context. "Stories are never innocent of point of view, plot, ideology, or cultural values. We tell our stories of the past in a historical context, looking at the past from a particular point: the present. We cannot be objective, neutral observers . . . Our views of the past are also affected by our geographical, political, and social location."[53] This is why interpretation is so

---

[53]Philip R. Davies, *Memories of Ancient Israel: An Introduction to Biblical History—Ancient and Modern* (Louisville, KY: Westminster John Knox Press, 2008), 11.

critical. The one who interprets assumes power, while the one who dominates the story makes it their story. The more the story is remembered and repeated, the easier it is to develop into a mythical history. This is the struggle when dealing today with the notion of election.

A Faith Perspective

The Bible is a story of people with God. It is not an objective observation or investigation about God. It is a perspective of faith and can be understood only from this angle. It cannot be objectified or seen from a distant perspective. The phenomenon of individuals or groups who view their story with God as unique and believe themselves to be chosen is one shared by all monotheistic religions. Pious Jews believe that they, or rather their people, are the chosen people (Exodus 19:5–6); pious Christians, on the other hand, believe that they have become the chosen people through Christ (1 Peter 2:9–10); Muslims have similar beliefs (Q3:110). One should respect and honor such an expression of faith, but one need not consider it to be an objective truth or a historic reality. The structures of faith are very like the structures of love. Just as a lover cannot help but see his or her beloved as "the one," unique and special, the "lily among the flowers," so a believer cannot do other than view his or her connectedness to God as unique and, to a certain degree, exclusive.

If this statement of faith is objectified or even absolutized by any particular individual or a group, it loses its rightful *Sitz im Leben* and develops into a dangerous ideology. There is a very thin line between faith and ideology. Christians believe that, without any effort on their part, God has chosen them through Christ. But this does not mean that they must immediately declare that they are the only chosen one and that "the others" are not chosen or are even rejected. Nor can they cultivate any kind of "objective" theological dogma about who is elected or not, or to be able to discern about the election or rejection of other people. We human beings in this world have no business determining who is or who is not chosen, or who is chosen and who is rejected. This is God's business. It does not mean that this does not happen. It occurs in the Bible, it has occurred over and over again in history, and it is taking place today. When this occurs, it is a sign of human and religious hubris that has no place in the realm of faith. Such hubris has more to do with ideology than with theology.

Particular versus Singular

While the biblical story is one particular story related to a certain time and place, it made history because of its relevance to the diverse contexts of imperial hegemonic oppression world-wide. In sharing their particular story (biblical story), many people facing imperial oppression were able to relate to this story and find meaning in the face of empire. The particularity of the story, however, does not mean singularity. This is why election can never be an entitlement to a particular land or people. In a context that faced empire, it was time for prophets to warn: "You only have I chosen among all the families of the earth; Therefore I will punish you for all your iniquities" (Amos 3:2; see also Hosea 13:4–8). Yet, this same prophet, Amos, who spoke these words about the particularity of election, was also the one to remind his people, saying on God's behalf, "Are you not like the Ethiopians to me, O people of Israel? says the Lord. Did I not bring Israel up from the land of Egypt, and the Philistines from Caphtor and Arameans from Kir?" (Amos 9:7). Amos shows that the Exodus was not a singular rescue involving only biblical Israel. God also dealt with the other branch of the people of Palestine, the Philistines, in a similar way and had a particular exodus story with the Arameans. God does not cease to be Creator and preserver of the whole world. The particularity of the biblical story with God does not mean that God had or has no interest in other peoples. The Prophet Isaiah underlined this by including in the story the two main empires surrounding Palestine: "In that day there will be a highway from Egypt to Assyria. The Assyrians will go to Egypt and the Egyptians to Assyria. The Egyptians and Assyrians will worship together. In that day Israel will be the third, along with Egypt and Assyria, a blessing on the earth. The Lord Almighty will bless them, saying, "Blessed be Egypt my people, Assyria my handiwork, and Israel my inheritance" (Isaiah 19:23–25).

This nuance between particularity and singularity is reconfirmed in the book of Jonah, when the prophet spoke to his people who thought that they had a monopoly over God's story and mercy. The Jonah story made it clear that God's plans encompass all the peoples of the world. God felt sorry for Nineveh, its inhabitants, yes, even the animals there (Jonah 4:11), even though Nineveh was the capital of the Assyrian Empire. The New Testament continued this trend and clearly showed that, although the story is particular, it cannot be understood as an entitlement. The essence of the story from its inception was meant to be an inclusive invitation to all people without exception. This is the question that Paul deals with in his letters and especially in Romans 9–11.[54]

It is important to underline that Paul deals in these three chapters with a personal struggle that he had as an apostle: the fact that his coreligionists did not believe in Christ. Ultimately, Paul interprets the essence of God's story as one that shows God's promise against all odds. Paul does not deal here with any speculation about the future. To read these chapters as a guide to the future is a fundamentalist interpretation. These three

---

[54]A detailed though older exegesies of Romans 9–11 can be found in Mitri Raheb, *I Am a Palestinian Christian* (Minneapolis: Fortress Press, 2009), 67–69.

chapters do not deal with the relationship between Judaism and Christianity or between the modern State of Israel and the church. This is an imposition on the text. If there is one lesson that this text teaches us, it is that election is God's business, and no one has a monopoly over it. God's salvation surpasses all understanding, and God remains the God of surprises that all our theological systems cannot contain.

A Geopolitical Perspective

Christian dogma will not help us understand the *Sitz im Leben* of the notion of election, for the biblical story cannot be understood outside of its contexts and its geopolitical settings. In this section, I further develop work that I have previously published in *Faith in the Face of Empire: The Bible through Palestinian Eyes.*[55]

In the middle of the second millennium BC, two major centers of power evolved in the Middle East. Their development was closely connected to geography and water: at one end there was the Nile, and on the other, there were two rivers: the Tigris and Euphrates. At approximately the same time and in close proximity, three other regional powers were developing the boundaries of the region: Persia/Iran to the east, Hittites/Turkey to the north, and Greco–Roman Europe to the west. The history of the region over the last three millennia shows that the Middle East was controlled for most of the time by one of these five empires, albeit with different names, constellations, and degrees of power.[56] The small strip between the Mediterranean and the Jordan River known as Palestine was too small and lacked the geographical location and resources

---

[55]Mitri Raheb, *Faith in the Face of Empire: The Bible through Palestinian Eyes* (Maryknoll, NY: Orbis Books, 2014).

[56]Ibid., 43–47.

to develop into an empire. Palestine was located between these other empires, its fate dictated by its geography as a land in the eye of the storm. The people of Palestine were aware of this geopolitical reality: "This is Jerusalem; I have set her at the center of the nations, with lands around her" (Ezekiel 5:5); "Behold, a people who dwells apart, and will not be reckoned among the nations" (Numbers 23:5).

As discussed in the previous chapter, Palestine's location between five empires does not necessarily make it the center. In fact, the opposite is true: Palestine is a land at the periphery, a land on the margins. Contrary to its religious reputation, in its geopolitical reality, the land lies on the periphery of the Fertile Crescent and is a peripheral borderland for diverse empires, making Palestine the location where the different magnetic fields of the regional powers would collide. Situated between different empires, the fertile plains of Palestine often became the battlefield for the surrounding empires to keep their wars and tragedies away from their heartlands. Due to its geopolitical position between powers, Palestine has often been an occupied land: occupied by the Egyptians, Assyrians, Babylonians, Persians, Greeks, Romans, Byzantines, Arabs, Crusaders, Ottomans, British, and now by the Israelis.[57]

This is the background behind the notion of election. It is not by chance that the verses that deal with election were developed mainly in the context of the Assyrian and Babylonian occupation and exile: in Deuteronomy and the Deuteronomic literature, in Deutero-Isaiah, and in the Psalms. The verb used for election *(bahar)* first appeared as late as the sixth century, although the concept itself might be older. It is when Palestine was devastated and burned down; when the empires were proving triumphant over the tiny political structure in Palestine; when the imperial Gods were celebrating their victory over

---

[57]Ibid., 49–54.

the God of the people of Palestine, be it Israelites or Judeans; when everything seemed to be lost and the spirit of the people crushed, two different religious explanations emerged. The first explanation declared that the defeat was not so much an indication of foreign imperial power, but rather a sign that God had abandoned and rejected God's people because of their sins. We find this especially in the book of the prophet Jeremiah: "They call them rejected silver, because the Lord has rejected them" (Jeremiah 6:30); "I have forsaken My house, I have abandoned My inheritance; I have given the beloved of My soul into the hand of her enemies" (Jeremiah 7:12).

Yet, in this same context of devastation, another explanation was given. Other prophets felt that what people needed was comfort and hope. It is here that the notion of *election was evoked* with the aim of restoring people's hope in themselves over and against the tragic political reality they were experiencing. We see this clearly in the book of Deutero-Isaiah, the prophet in exile who wrestles with the desperate:

> But Zion said, "The Lord has forsaken me, my Lord has forgotten me." Can a woman forget her nursing child, or show no compassion for the child of her womb? Even these may forget, yet I will not forget you. See, I have inscribed you on the palms of my hands; your walls are continually before me. (Isaiah 49:14–16)

and

> But you, Israel, my servant, Jacob, whom I have chosen, the offspring of Abraham, my friend; you whom I took from the ends of the earth, and called from its farthest corners, saying to you, "You are my servant, I have chosen you and not cast you off"; do not fear, for I am with you, do not be afraid, for I am your God; I will strengthen you, I

will help you, I will uphold you with my victorious right hand. (Isaiah 41:8–10)

Election was and will always be a statement of faith; it is solely a promise. It is a promise to those weak and powerless, to those who begin to despair about themselves. It is to them that election is proclaimed. This is the *Sitz im Leben* of the notion of election. Election is connected to the balance of power. Election, correctly understood, is therefore a promise to those crushed by imperial power, encouragement to those discouraged by the political realities, and consolation to the desperate, as seen in the book of Deuteronomy:

> For you are a holy people to the Lord your God; the Lord your God has chosen you to be a people for His own possession out of all the peoples who are on the face of the earth. The Lord did not set His love on you nor choose you because you were more in number than any of the peoples, for you were the fewest of all peoples, but because the Lord loved you and kept the oath which He swore to your forefathers, the Lord brought you out by a mighty hand and redeemed you from the house of slavery, from the hand of Pharaoh king of Egypt. (Deuteronomy 7:6–8)

It is with a notion like election that the people of Palestine were able to face the diverse imperial occupations throughout millennia. Such faith generated so much power that it enabled the people of Palestine to be resilient and to survive against almost impossible odds. When everything had fallen apart and nothing seemed to have any meaning, it was this notion of election that enabled the people of Palestine to survive and resist the diverse imperial oppressions they were facing.

This was not the only *Sitz im Leben* for the notion of election. Palestine was often a divided land and stood in the sphere of influence of two of the five empires simultaneously, which led naturally to having the land divided into two or more entities. This was the case, for example, when the Assyrians occupied the northern part of Palestine, leaving some distance from Egypt's sphere of influence in the south. After the Assyrian occupation, two different identities developed in Palestine: one in the northern part where the people later became known as Samaritans, and another in the south where the people became known as Judeans. In this context, the notion of election was weaponized to give one group, mainly the Judeans, religious entitlement over and against the Samaritans: the temple of Jerusalem against the Samaritan temple on Gerizim (John 4:20). While there were many places of worship and religious cults in Palestine throughout centuries, many of them going back to Canaanite religions, election became a tool for religious and exclusive national hegemony that does not tolerate any alternative with the notion that God has chosen Jerusalem as God's place of worship (Deuteronomy 12—18). This notion of election is the other feature of Deuteronomy–Deuteronomic literature.

Thus, it is important to always keep in mind these two different and opposed religious utilizations of the notion of election: one as a message of hope for the weak and devastated, and one as a tool for religious and national ideology. These two opposing interpretations cannot be identified from a biblical or dogmatic approach to the issue but through a geopolitical lens and analysis of the prevailing balance of power. Today, the State of Israel has developed to become the regional power, an empire in proxy. The Palestinians now live in a situation similar to the Israelites of the Bible: occupied, crushed, their children driven into exile, and left with little land and no resources. When the notion of election is applied today to the State of Israel, it runs contrary to its original *Sitz im Leben* and has developed into an imperial tool for oppression and dispossession. It is the Palestinians who often feel abandoned, who need to hear that God did not forsake them and that they continue to be a people dear to God's heart.

Reading the Story Backward

A major misunderstanding of the notion of election drives from the interpretation of the story of the patriarchs through the lens of *salvation history (Heilsgeschichte)*. Election here is understood as a continuous act of selection (Genesis 12—50). Abraham had two sons: Ishmael the first born, the son of Hagar, and Isaac, Sarah's son. Yet, Isaac becomes the chosen one and the only elected one while the story of Ishmael more or less ends here. The story continues through Isaac and gets even more complicated. Isaac has twins: Esau and Jacob. Here another selection takes place and Jacob becomes the bearer of the promise rather than Esau his twin. Of Jacob's twelve sons, Yosef was the preferred one who rose to power. This is how the biblical story of the patriarchs is told and retold, as a continuous process of election and selection leading to preferential treatment of one and biblical disqualification of the other. What happens to the theology of election if we read this story backward while looking at the geopolitics of Palestine? Doing so will free us from a literal understanding of the story and allow us to realize that the people of Palestine were negotiating their relationships.

The three patriarchs (Abraham, Isaac, and Jacob) represented diverse traditions and identities from three regions that were not necessarily connected (Abraham in the Negev, Isaac in Beersheba, and Jacob in Bethel and Samaria).[58] The story casts them in a father–son relationship, thus uniting the different tribes and regions of Palestine together in one single story of three generations and constituting a unity among the diverse

---

[58]See Mitri Raheb, "Land, Voelker und Identitaeten; ein palaestinensischer Standpunkt," *Concilium* 43, no. 2 (2007): 174–81.

peoples of Palestine. At the same time, the story wants to clarify the relationships to the neighboring tribes and regions. So, in Jordan, east of Palestine, resides the group of Lot. The story includes Lot not as a foreigner but as a relative, Abraham's nephew and a neighbor (Genesis 12:5). The story of Ishmael negotiates the relationship with the tribes in the southern part of the Sinai Peninsula (Genesis 21:21). They are not foreigners because Ishmael is also Abraham's son. The same is true for Esau, whose tribe resides in Edom, southeast of Palestine. He too is a relative, the brother of Isaac. Those do not reside in Palestine and are thus not considered part of the (elected) people of Palestine, but they are related. This reading of the story leads to a different conclusion, a conclusion that is less about selection and rejection and more about the struggle to unite the different tribes in Palestine while at the same time negotiating the relationships with the tribes around Palestine. A geopolitical reading of the story of the patriarchs opens up the possibility of including rather than excluding groups, tribes, and peoples.

The Continuation of the Story in the Quran[59]

The story of the patriarchs continues beyond the Bible. An interesting critique of election as a continuous story of selection and exclusion is found in the Quran. As long as Prophet Muhammad hoped that the Jews of Mecca might still believe in him, Ishmael was a prophet without any importance (Q6:86; Q21:85). However, in Medina, it became clear to Muhammad that the Jews of Medina would not believe in his message. They were proud to be the "chosen people" and claimed the *story*

---

[59]In this section, I closely mirror my article: Mitri Raheb, "Contextualising the Scripture: Towards a New Understanding of the Qur'an—An Arab-Christian Perspective," *Studies in World Christianity* 3, no. 2 (1997): 180–201, https://doi.org/10.3366/swc.1997.3.2.180.

that runs from Abraham through Isaac and Jacob exclusively for themselves. They considered the Arabs as the descendants of Ishmael and playing only a marginal role in the history of salvation. The Jews in Medina, in our terms, claimed the story as history and wrote Ishmael out of it.

Prophet Muhammad took up the cause of the excluded and marginalized represented by Ishmael by rescuing Ishmael from the shadows of the linear salvation history and making him equal with Isaac and Jacob (Q2:136; Q3:84). In the context of his dispute with the Jews (and Christians), and in an effort to clarify who Abraham's descendants were, Muhammad reverted to the religion of Abraham: "They [the People of the Book] say: You have to be a Jew or a Christian if you are to be on the path [of salvation]. Say: No! [For us there is only] the religion of Abraham, a *hanif*, who was not one of the idolaters" (Q2:135). By reverting to the religion of Abraham, Prophet Muhammad is critiquing the claim of exclusivity of the Jews and Christians and their monopoly over the story. Muhammad uses an argument similar to that of Paul in Romans 4 and Galatians 3 by reverting to Abrahamic faith (Genesis 15) that preceded his circumcision (Genesis 17). For Prophet Muhammad, election does not run exclusively through the line of Isaac and Jacob (as believed by Jews and Christians), but rather equally through Ishmael, and through him to the Arabs. This is demonstrated in Abraham's prayer at the *Ka'ba*: "Lord, send them (i.e., the descendants of Abraham and Ishmael) a messenger from their own ranks who will recite Your signs (revealed verses) to them, who will instruct them in the scripture and wisdom, and purify them (from the pollution of paganism). You are the Almighty and the All-wise" (Q2:129). Prophet Muhammad is thus elected with a clear mission: to include the descendants of Ishmael in God's story. Muhammad was able to elevate the Arabs and his followers to become equal with the Jews of his time.

Conclusion

Election is an important theological *topos*. Traditionally, theologians dealt with it from the perspective of the *history of salvation*. This approach led to misunderstandings, prejudices, and exclusive theologies that had and continue to have disastrous implications for the Palestinians, particularly Palestinian Christians who continue to struggle with it today. It is imperative to develop new approaches to election that are inclusive and that take the geopolitical context of the text and its *Wirkungsgeschichte* seriously. Election cannot be an innocent exercise in theological semantics but must include analysis of its sociopolitical and cultural manifestation. Election should not constitute a theological premise for a political claim.

For people of faith to believe that they are elected by God is one thing; to use this belief as a pretext for supremacy or entitlement to occupy other people's land is not permissible. Violations of human rights in the name of "divine right" should not be tolerated. Election is a statement of faith. Otherwise, it becomes a dangerous ideology that sanctions religiously based nationalism, settler colonialism, and racial exceptionalism with disastrous ramifications. Palestinians and many other indigenous peoples are paying the price of this ideology. When it is understood correctly, election has the potential to give hope to the marginalized and to offer much-needed support for creative resilience.

Epilogue

Throughout the past hundred years, Israel has used different means to further its settler colonial project: sometimes through conquest and land colonization, other times through illegal laws or economic pressures. Throughout these years, biblical mythistory has provided a discourse that depicted the native Palestinian Arabs as aliens or savage terrorists and the Jews as civilized, democratic, or a start-up nation. To defend the settler colonial project, Israel created a police state that was granted extraordinary power over the native people. The ultimate goal for Israel has been to control the whole geography of historic Palestine while confining the Palestinian population into different forms of Bantustans as an interim stage toward ultimate ethnic cleansing. Behind all of these endeavors lies a settler colonial mind-set and policy platform.

While some churches in Canada, Australia, and certain parts of the United States are confronting their own settler colonial heritage, Israel is advancing its settler colonial project at a rapid pace. These churches now acknowledge that they stand on land belonging to First Nations whereas Israeli settlers and colonizers are grabbing land from defenseless Palestinian families throughout the West Bank, in Massafer Yatta in the southern Hebron hills, in Yanun in the Nablus Governorate, and from Arab al-Jahalin in East Jerusalem. The story of Sheikh Jarrah is a story of settler colonialism and the replacement of the native people with new colonizers. The Judaization of Jerusalem is a story of settler colonialism that aims to erase the Arab and Palestinian presence from the city. The story of al-Aqsa is a story of settler colonialism in which the goal is to replace an Arab Muslim shrine and worshippers with a "third Jewish temple." The Israeli *hasbara* apparatus—roughly translated as the explanatory structure for the State of Israel—works to perpetuate the image of Palestinians as terrorists whose rockets deliberately kill civilians while Israeli airstrikes are conducted with "surgical precision," even if fifty or more Palestinian children are bombed "by mistake." All of these activities are based on a biblical discourse that gives the settlers the requisite theological rationale. This Israeli settler colonial endeavor has to be seen as the last chapter of the Western settler colonial project, taking place today in the twenty-first century in Palestine. It continues to be serviced and powered by the motherland: the Anglo-Saxon world.

The Empire at Work

The State of Israel must be seen as an integral part of empire or empire-by-proxy. The colonization of Palestine in modern history was facilitated by the British Empire through the Balfour Declaration and continues to be made possible by the American empire. In this sense, the imperial project that started in the mid-nineteenth century continues today. Today, empire is bigger than one state, nation, or military power. The Accra Confession defined empire as the convergence of economic, political, cultural, geographic, and military imperial interests, systems, and networks that seek to dominate political power and economic wealth.[1] Empire typically forces and facilitates the flow of wealth and power from vulnerable persons, communities, and countries

---

[1] World Communion of Reformed Churches, "The Accra Confession," 2004, http://wcrc.ch/accra/the-accra-confession.

to the more powerful. Empire today is linked to both Western hegemony that built its wealth over centuries of colonialism and to a vast military–industrial complex. Furthermore, empire today is linked to the so-called Judeo-Christian tradition that became a code for cultural and ethnic supremacy.

Israel is part of this empire and is sustained by it with supplies of "hardware" such as submarines, F35 fighter jets, the Iron Dome, and political backing. Israel is seen as part of the Western world, serving their interests as one of their main allies. Today, Israel is the seventh biggest exporter of military and security equipment worldwide. Additionally, the empire provides Israel with the "software" of a biblical blueprint that paints colonial practices with theological justifications of a "promised land" and "chosen people." The software further depicts Israel as a shining example of the so-called democratic world and Western values.

The Ecumenical Deal

The Jewish liberation theologian Marc Ellis coined the phrase *the ecumenical deal* to describe the relationship between the Jewish synagogue and Christian church in the West. This ecumenical deal is usually referred to as interfaith ecumenical dialogue, the post-Holocaust place where Jews and Christians have mended their relationship. Israel has been a critical influence in this dialogue. Christians supported Israel as repentance for anti-Semitism and the Holocaust. As Israel became more controversial due to its abuse of Palestinians, Christians remained silent. Failure to support—or worse, criticism of—Israeli policies was viewed by the Jewish dialoguers as a return to anti-Semitism. The dialogue became a deal: silence on the part of Christians earns no criticism of anti-Semitism from Jews. The interfaith ecumenical deal was also part of a larger political deal in the American political scene. Any criticism of Israel by a political figure was their death knell, and accusations of anti-Semitism were the bullets.[2]

In 2012, Marc Ellis declared this ecumenical deal dead. While several mainline Protestant churches like the Presbyterian Church USA and the United Church of Christ are today more articulate than ever, most of the mega and influential congregations in the main American cities are sticking to the ecumenical deal just as it is still alive and even thriving in many European countries like Germany, Holland, and even the human rights champion country, Sweden.

What is true for the churches is true for mainline Protestant theology. As Julia M. O'Brien puts it,

> For typical US mainline Protestants, an interpretation of a biblical text is *convincing and compelling* if they hear it as:
>
> - Liberal, supporting universal human rights, especially for those whom they recognize as historically oppressed, and even more especially women.
> - Scientific, objectively verified by text itself, even more by historians and archeologists.
> - Savvy, sufficiently skeptical of human bias.
> - Supportive of Judaism and supported by Jewish readers.
>
> An interpretation is *problematic* if they hear it as:
>
> - Socially conservative, unconcerned with the improvement of this world, especially the status of women.

---

[2]"Exile and the Prophetic: The Interfaith Ecumenical Deal Is Dead," Mondoweiss, November 12, 2012, https://mondoweiss.net/2012/11/exile-and-the-prophetic-the-interfaith-ecumenical-deal-is-dead/.

- Fundamentalist or overly pious, accepting biblical testimony at face value.
- Ideological, promoting only one side of a conflict that they believe is multi-faceted.
- Challenging what Jews say about the Old Testament.[3]

This hermeneutics has led to a Judaization of Christian theological writings and literature. While it was important to combat the earlier anti-Jewish traditions in Christian theology, the pro-Jewish hermeneutics created, consciously or unconsciously, a pro-Israeli attitude with an anti-Palestinian twist embedded in it. The Judaization of Christian theology ran parallel to the Judaization of the land of Palestine and, in some cases, provided a theological cushion for Israeli practices. Western views of Ashkenazi Israelis as members of their kin and of their own White tribe in the decades following the Holocaust further demonstrate the breadth of the theological commitment to settler colonial imperialism. The settler colonial narrative that celebrates the colonizers while criminalizing the natives as savages was particularly apparent in the film industry. Jack Shaheen, a scholar who dedicated his career to analyzing stereotypes in Hollywood films, examined over 1,100 films for his groundbreaking book *Reel Bad Arab: How Hollywood Vilifies a People* and found that Americans were entertained by anti-Arab, anti-Palestinian, and anti-Muslim propaganda.[4]

---

[3]Julia O'Brien, "The Hermeneutical Predicament: Why We Do Not Read the Bible in the Same Way and Why It Matters to Palestinian Advocacy," in *The Biblical Text in the Context of Occupation: Towards a New Hermeneutics of Liberation*, ed. Mitri Raheb (Bethlehem: Diyar, 2012), 169–70.

[4]Jack G. Shaheen, *Reel Bad Arabs: How Hollywood Vilifies a People*, 3rd ed. (Northampton, MA: Olive Branch Press, 2012).

History and Power

Churches feel that they must side with Israel because of what happened to the Jews in Europe during the Holocaust. Their declared rationale is that they have learned a lesson from history. This assumption needs to be questioned. Yes, maybe the church has become sensitive to anti-Jewish traditions within it, but the church still feels more comfortable in siding with those in power. The Israel lobby is very strong and actively rewards those who follow them while punishing those who resist their settler colonial praxis. It remains very costly to side with the weak and oppressed, and the price can be one's career, reputation, and even life. Dietrich Bonhoeffer was part of a tiny confessing church who dared to challenge the powers of his time, and he paid with his life. While Bonhoeffer is widely celebrated, almost as a Protestant saint, very few dare to walk in his footsteps today and challenge the Israeli state and its lobbies embedded in church and society. What lessons are learned from history if churches and political groups are fearful of the Israel lobby and side with the powerful State of Israel against the oppressed Palestinian people?

Anti-Semitism

Churches work seriously to combat anti-Semitism. The word *anti-Semitism* was coined in the late nineteenth century to describe the demonization and discrimination of a whole Jewish population in Europe. This is demonization and discrimination that must be confronted just like Islamophobia and other forms of racism. However, for the past three decades, since 1991, the Israel lobby has attempted to impose a new definition of anti-Semitism that puts the State of Israel itself above any criticism. It launched an international campaign to criminalize any criticism of the State of Israel, discrediting any real resistance to Israel's colonization project, even if the resistance is clearly nonviolent. As a result, advocating for Palestinian rights is criminalized as "hate speech." The space for prophetic witness, nonviolent resistance, and civic action is shrinking, and, with it, the right to free speech. This is particularly evident in Germany, where journalists and church and state officials are banned from using words like "apartheid" or "settler colonialism" in regard to the State of Israel.[5] Palestinian theologians are banned from preaching in German churches, human rights activists are disinvited, and access to lecture halls is forbidden to them. There is no break with history here; this is the continuation of the same old pattern of churches siding with those in power, in this case the Israel lobby in Germany, to censor the speech of those who are powerless and to ban them from the public sphere by various means.

The Two-State Solution

For many churches and politicians that side with Israel, the simplest way to do so is to show support for a two-state solution with an Israeli state on 77 percent of historic Palestine side by side with a Palestinian state on the remaining 23 percent. For politicians and church officials who want to play it safe, the answer is to endorse the vision of a two-state solution. The international community pays lip service to the two-state solution despite recognizing that the settler colonial project

---

[5]Ben Knight, "Lawmakers Condemn 'Anti-Semitic' BDS Movement," *DW.com*, May 17, 2019, https://www.dw.com/en/german-parliament-condemns-anti-semitic-bds-movement/a-48779516; Hebh Jamal, "Germany Is Targeting Post-colonial Thinkers for a Reason," *Al Jazeera English*, December 12, 2022.

is eating away at the Palestinian state slowly but surely. Many politicians are aware that it is already too late for a two-state solution, yet they continue to show allegiance to it. While it is, indeed, too late for a two-state solution, it is also too early for a one-state solution while the international community continues to espouse the two-state paradigm rather than confronting the settler colonial approach of Israel. Several political models for a just and peaceful solution exist: a federation, a confederation, or a Swiss model of cantons in which each canton preserves its own cultural identity while cherishing the unity of the people and country. It is not the model that is lacking but the will to end the settler colonial project. Without an end to the Israeli settler colonial project, the entire country is stuck in a situation best described as apartheid.

Apartheid

Many years ago, credible politicians like President Jimmy Carter warned that, without a real peace agreement, the Israeli occupation would lead to an apartheid system.[6] President Carter was followed by Israeli politicians who rang similar alarms.[7] In the last two years, several highly credible human rights organizations, including Jewish human rights organizations like B'Tselem, have declared that the threshold has been crossed and that apartheid now exists on both sides of the Green Line.[8] Al-

---

[6]Jimmy Carter, *Palestine: Peace Not Apartheid*, reprint ed. (New York: Simon & Schuster, 2007).

[7]"Ehud Barak Warns: Israel Faces 'Slippery Slope' toward Apartheid," Israel News—Haaretz.com, https://www.haaretz.com/israel-news/2017-06-21/ty-article/ehud-barak-warns-israel-on-slippery-slope-to-apartheid/0000017f-ef8b-d0f7-a9ff-efcf52ce0000.

[8]B'Tselem, "Apartheid," accessed January 29, 2021, https://www.btselem.org/topic/apartheid.

though human rights organizations, like Human Rights Watch and Amnesty International, have identified the situation in historic Palestine as apartheid, the definition of apartheid was set by the Geneva Conventions, the International Convention on the Suppression and Punishment of the Crime of Apartheid, and the Rome Statute of the International Criminal Court.[9] Three decisive elements define the crime of apartheid: the implementation of a system of segregation based on race, religion, or ethnicity designed with the intent to maintain domination by one group over another; the use of diverse legislative measures to enforce and legalize segregation; and inhumane practices and violations to impose and enforce such segregation. These three components are also found in the definition of settler colonialism. Apartheid and settler colonialism are two sides of the same coin.

Peace Building

While churches and politicians pay lip service to a two-state solution, humanitarian organizations are engaged in providing Palestinians with humanitarian aid as if the issue at stake were a humanitarian crisis. The situation in Palestine is not a natural catastrophe but a man-made or state-made catastrophe. Palestinians are not hungry for bread but for rights. In fact, the total amount of aid injected into Palestine is less than the actual costs to Palestinians of Israeli restrictions on the movement of goods and people, and access to agricultural land, water, and resources. Meanwhile, nongovernmental organizations imple-

---

[9]Omar Shakir, "Israeli Apartheid: 'A Threshold Crossed,'" July 19, 2021, https://www.hrw.org/news/2021/07/19/israeli-apartheid-threshold-crossed; Amnesty International, "Israel's Apartheid against Palestinians," February 1, 2022, https://www.amnesty.org/en/latest/campaigns/2022/02/israels-system-of-apartheid/.

ment peace-building programs that are far from innocent. Mandy Turner, prominent international scholar and professor of conflict, peace, and humanitarian affairs at the University of Manchester in the United Kingdom, convincingly argues that Western peace building has been ultimately conceptualized with a colonial mind-set.[10] One aspect of this colonial peace building is a modern version of *mission civilisatrice*.[11] Peace building comprises preparing Palestinians for self-governance and state building through "good governance" programs while rehabilitating the Palestinian economy for entry into the free market economy.[12] This was a colonial practice implemented in many countries placed under mandate after WWI to prepare them for statehood, while simultaneously ensuring that the emerging state would maintain colonial interests. In the case of Palestine, the aim was to serve Israeli interests.

Security

Security is the top Israeli priority. An important aspect of colonial peace building in Palestine was, therefore, counterinsurgency.[13] The Palestinian resistance was depicted as brutal and requiring pacification by "securing" the Palestinian population and ensuring acquiescence in the face of violent settler colonial dispossession. One-third of the budget provided by the donor

---

[10]Mandy Turner, "Completing the Circle: Peacebuilding as Colonial Practice in the Occupied Palestinian Territory," *International Peacekeeping* 19, no. 4 (2012): 492–507.

[11]Roland Paris, "International Peacebuilding and the 'Mission Civilisatrice,'" *Review of International Studies* 28, no. 4 (2002): 637–56.

[12]M. Pugh, N. Cooper, and M. Turner, eds., *Whose Peace? Critical Perspectives on the Political Economy of Peacebuilding* (Houndmills, Basingstoke, UK: Palgrave Macmillan, 2008).

[13]Mandy Turner, "Peacebuilding as Counterinsurgency in the Occupied Palestinian Territory," *Review of International Studies* 41, no. 1 (2015): 1–26.

community went into building the Palestinian security forces, and there is now one security agent for every seventy-five Palestinians, one of the highest ratios in the world. This heavy investment in Palestinian security was less about security for the Palestinian people and more to provide security for Israel and its settler colonies. Donor investments given to the Palestinian Authority were really intended for Israel's security. The characteristic settler colonial creation of a police state to control the native colonized population is executed both directly by Israeli military forces and through a proxy, the Palestinian security forces. In this way, peace building in the occupied Palestinian territories succeeded in silencing any credible resistance among the Palestinian population to the Israeli settler colonial project. Even nonviolent resistance, such as boycott, divestment, and sanctions (BDS), is discredited by the donor community while decolonial Palestinian theologies are avoided by churches and their hierarchies.

Toward a Paradigm Shift

The same Western politicians and church leaders who shy away from supporting Palestine and criminalize Palestinian resistance are mobilizing political, financial, public relations, and military power in support of Ukraine against Russia. While they perceive the 2022 Russian invasion as a clear-cut act of atrocity that requires support for the Ukrainian people, they describe the Israeli occupation of Palestinian land as *complicated*, ignoring the clarity of the case in international law. The description *complicated* is used to blur the Palestinian issue, portraying it as an exception to the rule. Palestine presents a real challenge to the credibility of the entire Western world, a world that has not yet come to terms with the ramifications of its colonial heritage.

Unfortunately, there is no indication that this will change

in the short term. The West will continue to provide their ally with military hardware and theological software. The State of Israel is the seventh largest military power worldwide, and the Jewish lobby is investing billions of dollars to silence voices that oppose the settler colonial project. They do not feel any urgency or reason to compromise. On the contrary, the Israeli establishment now sees an opportunity to seal its deal and bring its settler colonial project to its ultimate completion.

Yet, some cracks in the wall are visible, and the Israeli settler colonial project is failing. Today in historic Palestine, there is an equal number of Palestinians to Israeli Jews, and all Palestinians, irrespective of where they live and under which jurisdiction (within the Green Line, in the West Bank, East Jerusalem, Gaza, or in the diaspora), have recognized the real intentions and nature of the settler colonial project. Palestinians will not disappear from the land where their roots lie. We continue to demonstrate unity across artificial borders and determination to resist the settler colonial project with all available means. There is a young and dynamic generation of Palestinians who are articulate, passionate, skilled, and active in defending their cause. If the name of the game for Israelis is settler colonialism, the name of the game for Palestinians is resilience: *sumud*. For more than seventy years, Palestinians have faithfully shown a tremendous strength to resist, incredible forms of resilience, and creative ways to survive. The Palestinians are not moving, and they will persist in the face of the Israeli settler colonial project.

The Israeli settler colonial project constitutes a threat to Palestinians and to the many Jews who desire to live in peace with the Palestinians. While the peace camp in Israel has shrunk tremendously, Jewish groups in the diaspora like Jewish Voices for Peace have recognized the harm that the Israeli settler colonial project is doing to their Jewish identity and liberal outlook. They do not want to associate with the policies and settler colonial practices of the "Jewish State." They declare freely and unapologetically their solidarity and support for an end to the settler colonial project. Solidarity networks have been created with social justice movements like Black Lives Matter, with artists from the First Nations, Indigenous Americans, and Aboriginal Peoples. Conferences focusing on Palestinian contextual theology are taking place in many locations.

Will this bring about the desired change soon? I doubt it! Yet, all these steps will continue to widen the cracks in the wall until the day that it will fall. I have no doubt that all walls will fall. There is no future for this settler colonial project. Palestine must be understood as one of the last anti-colonial struggles in an era regarded as post-colonial. This book is an urgent call to decolonize Christian theology regarding the Palestinian land and its people, to understand Israel through a new paradigm of settler colonialism, and to contribute to the struggle for liberation, human dignity, and justice.

Selected Bibliography

Abu El-Assal, Riah. *Caught in Between: The Story of an Arab Palestinian Christian Israeli.* London: SPCK, 1999.

Ahlstrom, Gosta W., and Gary O. Rollefson. *The History of Ancient Palestine.* Edited by Diana Edelman. Minneapolis: Fortress Press, 1993.

Alazzeh, Ala. "Seeking Popular Participation: Nostalgia for the First Intifada in the West Bank." *Settler Colonial Studies* 5, no. 3 (2015): 251–67.

Ateek, Naim Stifan. *A Palestinian Christian Cry for Reconciliation.* Maryknoll, NY: Orbis Books, 2008.

——. *Justice, and Only Justice: A Palestinian Theology of Liberation.* Maryknoll, NY: Orbis Books, 1989.

Ateek, Naim Stifan, Cedar Duaybis, and Maurine Tobin. *Challenging Christian Zionism: Theology, Politics and the Israel-Palestine Conflict.* London: Melisende, 2005.

Ateek, Naim Stifan, Marc H. Ellis, and Rosemary Radford Ruether. *Faith and the Intifada: Palestinian Christian Voices.* Maryknoll, NY: Orbis Books, 1992.

Ateek, Naim Stifan, and Michael Prior, *Holy Land, Hollow Jubilee: God, Justice, and the Palestinians.* London: Melisende, 1999.

Badarin, Emile. "Settler-Colonialist Management of Entrances to the Native Urban Space in Palestine." *Settler Colonial Studies* 5, no. 3 (2015): 226–35.

Banner, Stuart. *How the Indians Lost Their Land: Law and Power on the Frontier.* Cambridge, MA: Belknap Press: An Imprint of Harvard University Press, 2007.

————. *Possessing the Pacific: Land, Settlers, and Indigenous People from Australia to Alaska.* Cambridge, MA: Harvard University Press, 2007.

Barth, Markus. *Der Jude Jesus, Israel und die Palästinenser.* Zürich: TVZ-Verlag, 1975.

————. *Jesus the Jew: What Does It Mean That Jesus Is a Jew?: Israel and the Palestinians.* Atlanta, GA: John Knox Press, 1978.

Bateman, F., and L. Pilkington, eds. *Studies in Settler Colonialism: Politics, Identity and Culture.* Houndsmill, Basingstoke, UK: Palgrave Macmillan, 2011.

Ben-Ephraim, Shaiel. "Do unto Others as They Have Done unto You: Explaining the Varying Tragic Outcomes of Settler Colonialism." *Settler Colonial Studies* 5, no. 3 (2015): 236–50.

Beška, Emanuel. "Anti-Zionist Journalistic Works of Najib Al-Khouri Nassar in the Newspaper Al-Karmel in 1914." *Asian and African Studies* 20 (2011): 167–92.

————. "Political Opposition to Zionism in Palestine and Greater Syria: 1910–1911 as a Turning Point." *Jerusalem Quarterly* 59 (2014): 54–67.

————. "The Anti-Zionist Attitudes and Activities of Ruhi al-Khalidi," in *Arabic and Islamic Studies in Honour of Ján Pauliny.* Ed. Gažáková Zuzana and Jaroslav Drobný. Bratislava: Comenius University in Bratislava, 2016, 181–203.

Brueggemann, Walter. *The Land.* Overtures to Biblical Theology. Philadelphia: Fortress Press, 1977.

————. *The Land: Place as Gift, Promise, and Challenge in Biblical Faith.* 2nd ed. Overtures to Biblical Theology. Minneapolis: Fortress Press, 2002.

B'Tselem. "Statistics on Settlements and Settler Population." https://www.btselem.org/settlements/statistics.

————. "The Occupied Territories and International Law." https://www.btselem.org/international_law.

Buck, Mary Ellen. *The Canaanites: Their History and Culture from Texts and Artifacts*. Eugene, OR: Cascade Books, 2019.

Burge, Gary M. *Jesus and the Land: The New Testament Challenge to "Holy Land" Theology*. Grand Rapids: Baker Academic, 2010.

———. *The Bible and the Land: Uncover the Ancient Culture, Discover Hidden Meanings*. Ancient Context, Ancient Faith. Grand Rapids: Zondervan, 2009.

———. *Whose Land? Whose Promise?: What Christians Are Not Being Told about Israel and the Palestinians*. Cleveland: Pilgrim Press, 2003.

Carter, Jimmy. *Palestine: Peace Not Apartheid*. Reprint ed. New York: Simon & Schuster, 2007.

Carter, Warren. *Matthew and Empire: Initial Explorations*. Harrisburg, PA: Trinity Press International, 2001.

———. *The Roman Empire and the New Testament: An Essential Guide*. Abingdon Essential Guides. Nashville, TN: Abingdon Press, 2006.

Cavanagh, Edward, ed. *The Routledge Handbook of the History of Settler Colonialism*. London: Routledge, 2020.

Chacour, Elias. *Blood Brothers*. Tarrytown, NY: Chosen Books, 1984.

———. *We Belong to the Land: The Story of a Palestinian Israeli Who Lives for Peace and Reconciliation*. San Francisco: HarperSanFrancisco, 1992.

Coogan, Michael D., and Mark S. Smith, eds. *Stories from Ancient Canaan*. 2nd ed. Louisville, KY: Westminster John Knox Press, 2012.

Davies, Philip R. *In Search of "Ancient Israel": A Study in Biblical Origins*. 2nd ed. New York: T&T Clark, 2015.

Davies, W. D. *The Territorial Dimension of Judaism*. Berkeley: University of California Press, 1982.

Day, David. *Conquest: How Societies Overwhelm Others*. Illustrated ed. Oxford: Oxford University Press, 2012.

Dayan, Moshe. *Living with the Bible*. New York: Bantam Books, 1979.

Drost, Andries H. "A Century of Interplay between Theology and Politics in Palestine—A Dutch Perspective." In *The Invention of History: A Century of Interplay between Theology and Politics in Palestine*, ed. Mitri Raheb, 33–58. Bethlehem: CreateSpace Independent Publishing Platform, 2011.

Eid, Xavier Abu. "Violations of the Law during COVID-19: Israeli Annexation Plans in Western Bethlehem." In *The Double Lockdown: Palestine under Occupation and COVID-19*, ed. Saeb Erakat and Mitri Raheb. Bethlehem: Diyar, 2020, 31–41.

El-Fadel, M., R. Quba'a, N. El-Hougeiri, Z. Hashisho, and D. Jamali. "The Israeli Palestinian Mountain Aquifer: A Case Study in Ground Water Conflict Resolution." *Journal of Natural Resources and Life Sciences Education* 30, no. 1 (2001): 50–61.

Elkins, Caroline, and Susan Pedersen, eds. *Settler Colonialism in the Twentieth Century: Projects, Practices, Legacies*. New York: Routledge, 2005.

Ellis, Marc H. *Israel and Palestine—Out of the Ashes: The Search for Jewish Identity in the Twenty-First Century*. London: Pluto Press, 2002.

———. *Judaism Does Not Equal Israel*. New York: New Press, 2009.

———. *Toward a Jewish Theology of Liberation: The Challenge of the 21st Century*. 3rd expanded ed. Waco, TX: Baylor University Press, 2004.

Erakat, Saeb, and Mitri Raheb, eds. *The Double Lockdown: Palestine under Occupation and COVID-19*. Bethlehem: Diyar, 2020.

"Final Text of Jewish Nation-State Law, Approved by the Knesset Early on July 19." *Times of Israel*. https://www.timesofisrael.com/final-text-of-jewish-nation-state-bill-set-to-become-law/.

Finkelstein, Israel. *The Quest for the Historical Israel: Archaeology and the History of Early Israel.* Atlanta, GA: Society of Biblical Literature, 2007.

"Full Transcript of Pence's Knesset Speech." *Jerusalem Post.* https://www.jpost.com/Israel-News/Full-transcript-of-Pences-Knesset-speech-539476.

Gaston, K. Healan. *Imagining Judeo-Christian America: Religion, Secularism, and the Redefinition of Democracy.* Chicago: University of Chicago Press, 2019.

Gush Etzion Foundation. "Gush Etzion." https://gush-etzion.org.il/.

Habel, Norman C. *Acknowledgment of the Land and Faith of Aboriginal Custodians after Following the Abraham Trail.* Eugene, OR: Wipf and Stock, 2018.

———. *The Land Is Mine: Six Biblical Land Ideologies.* Overtures to Biblical Theology. Minneapolis: Fortress Press, 1995.

Havrelock, Rachel. *The Joshua Generation: Israeli Occupation and the Bible.* Princeton, NJ: Princeton University Press, 2022.

Haynes, Stephen R. "Christian Holocaust Theology: A Critical Reassessment." *Journal of the American Academy of Religion* 62, no. 2 (1994): 553–85.

Herzl, Theodor. *The Complete Diaries of Theodor Herzl.* Ed. Raphael Patai. Trans. Harry Zohn. New York: Herzl Press, 1960.

Hjelm, Ingrid. "The Palestine History and Heritage Project (PaHH)." In *The Ever Elusive Past: Discussions of Palestine's History and Heritage,* 9–19. United Arab Emirates: Dar Al Nasher, 2019.

Hjelm, Ingrid, Hamdan Taha, Ilan Pappe, and Thomas L. Thompson, eds. *A New Critical Approach to the History of Palestine: Palestine History and Heritage Project 1.* London: Routledge, 2019.

Horsley, Richard A. *In the Shadow of Empire: Reclaiming the Bible as a History of Faithful Resistance.* Louisville, KY: Westminster John Knox Press, 2008.

————. *Jesus and the Politics of Roman Palestine.* Columbia: University of South Carolina Press, 2014.

————. *Jesus and the Powers: Conflict, Covenant, and the Hope of the Poor.* Minneapolis: Fortress Press, 2011.

————. *Paul and the Roman Imperial Order.* Harrisburg, PA.: Trinity Press International, 2004.

Ir Amim. "Annexation Moves Intensify: Greater Jerusalem Bill Hits Ministerial Committee on Legislation on Sunday," June 11, 2020. http://www.ir-amim.org.il/en/node/2121.

Isaac, Munther. *From Land to Lands; from Eden to the Renewed Earth: A Christ-Centred Biblical Theology of the Promised Land.* Carlisle, Cumbria, UK: Langham Monographs, 2015.

"Israeli Settlements and International Law." https://www.amnesty.org/en/latest/campaigns/2019/01/chapter-3-israeli-settlements-and-international-law/.

Jansen, Jan C., and Jürgen Osterhammel. *Decolonization: A Short History.* Trans. Jeremiah Riemer. Princeton, NJ: Princeton University Press, 2017.

Jasper, David. *A Short Introduction to Hermeneutics.* Louisville, KY: Westminster John Knox Press, 2004.

Kanʿān, Tawfiq. *Tawfiq Canaan: An Autobiography.* Ed. Mitri Raheb. Bethlehem: Diyar, 2020.

Katanacho, Yohanna. *The Land of Christ: A Palestinian Cry.* Eugene, OR: Wipf and Stock, 2013.

Khalidi, Rashid. *The Hundred Years' War on Palestine: A History of Settler Colonialism and Resistance, 1917–2017.* New York: Metropolitan Books, 2020.

Kickel, Walter. *Das gelobte Land: Die religiöse Bedeutung des Staates Israel in jüdischer und christlicher Sicht.* Munich: Kösel, 1984.

Kwok, Pui-lan. *Discovering the Bible in the Non-Biblical World.* Bible & Liberation. Maryknoll, NY: Orbis Books, 1995.

Latin Patriarchate of Jerusalem. "Fourth Pastoral Letter of Patriarch Sabbah, November 1993." https://www.lpj.org/archives/

fourth-pastoral-letter-patriarch-sabbah-reading-bible-today-land-bible-november-1993-5e45d3114195b.html.

Lemche, Niels Peter. *Ancient Israel: A New History of Israel.* 2nd ed. London: T&T Clark, 2015.

Liew, Tat-siong Benny. *Colonialism and the Bible: Contemporary Reflections from the Global South.* Lanham, MD: Lexington Books, 2018.

Loeffler, James. "The Problem with the 'Judeo-Christian Tradition.'" *The Atlantic,* August 1, 2020. https://www.theatlantic.com/ideas/archive/2020/08/the-judeo-christian-tradition-is-over/614812/.

Lubin, Alex, and Alyosha Goldstein. *Settler Colonialism.* Durham, NC: Duke University Press, 2008.

Mar, Tracey Banivanua, and P. Edmonds, eds. *Making Settler Colonial Space: Perspectives on Race, Place and Identity.* Houndmills, Basingstoke, UK: Palgrave Macmillan, 2010.

Marquardt, Friedrich Wilhelm. *Die Juden Und Ihr Land.* Gütersloh, Germany: Guetersloher Verlagshaus, 1993.

Masalha, Nur. *Expulsion of the Palestinians: The Concept of "Transfer" in Zionist Political Thought, 1882–1948.* Washington, DC: Institute for Palestine Studies, 1992.

———. *Imperial Israel and the Palestinians: The Politics of Expansion.* Sterling, VA: Pluto Press, 2000.

———. *Palestine: A Four-Thousand-Year History.* London: Zed Books, 2018.

———. *The Bible and Zionism: Invented Traditions, Archaeology and Post-Colonialism in Palestine-Israel.* London: Zed Books, 2007.

———. *The Palestine Nakba: Decolonising History, Narrating the Subaltern, Reclaiming Memory.* New York: Zed Books, 2012.

———. *The Politics of Denial: Israel and the Palestinian Refugee Problem.* London: Pluto Press, 2003.

Masalha, Nur, and Lisa Isherwood, eds. *Theologies of Liberation in Palestine-Israel.* Eugene, OR: Wipf and Stock, 2014.

Mein, Andrew, and Claudia V. Camp. *Far from Minimal: Celebrating the Work and Influence of Philip R. Davies.* Ed. Duncan Burns and John W. Rogerson. London: T&T Clark, 2012.

Moxnes, Halvor. *Jesus and the Rise of Nationalism: A New Quest for the Nineteenth-Century Historical Jesus.* London: IB Taurus, 2012.

Moxnes, Halvor, Ward Blanton, and James G. Crossley. *Jesus beyond Nationalism: Constructing the Historical Jesus in a Period of Cultural Complexity.* Bible World (London, England). London: Equinox, 2009.

Munayer, Salim, and Lisa Loden. *The Land Cries Out: Theology of the Land in the Israeli-Palestinian Context.* Eugene, OR: Cascade Books, 2012.

Nahla Abdo, and Nira Yuval-Davis. "Palestine, Israel and the Zionist Settler Project." In *Unsettling Settler Societies: Articulations of Gender, Race, Ethnicity and Class.* Ed. Daiva K. Stasiulis and Nira Yuval-Davis, 291–321. London: SAGE Publications, 1995.

New, David S. *Holy War: The Rise of Militant Christian, Jewish and Islamic Fundamentalism.* Jefferson, NC: McFarland, 2001.

Norris, Jacob. *Land of Progress: Palestine in the Age of Colonial Development, 1905–1948.* Oxford: Oxford University Press, 2013.

O'Brien, Julia. "The Hermeneutical Predicament: Why We Do Not Read the Bible in the Same Way and Why It Matters to Palestinian Advocacy." In *The Biblical Text in the Context of Occupation: Towards a New Hermeneutics of Liberation.* Ed. Mitri Raheb, 159–80. Bethlehem: Diyar, 2012.

Pagan, Samuel. "The Theological and Historical David: Contextual Reading." In *The Biblical Text in the Context of Occupation: Towards a New Hermeneutics of Liberation.* Ed. Mitri Raheb, 329–42. Bethlehem: Diyar, 2012.

Pappe, Ilan. *The Ethnic Cleansing of Palestine.* 2nd ed. London: Oneworld Publications, 2007.

Paris, Roland. "International Peacebuilding and the 'Mission Civilisatrice.'" *Review of International Studies* 28, no. 4 (2002): 637–56.

Pitkänen, Pekka. "Ancient Israel and Settler Colonialism." *Settler Colonial Studies* 4, no. 1 (2014): 64–81.

————. "Pentateuch–Joshua: A Settler-Colonial Document of a Supplanting Society." *Settler Colonial Studies* 4, no. 3 (2014): 245–76.

————. "Reading Genesis–Joshua as a Unified Document from an Early Date: A Settler Colonial Perspective." *Biblical Theology Bulletin*, February 3, 2015.

Prior, Michael. *Bible and Colonialism: A Moral Critique*. Sheffield, UK: Sheffield Academic Publishing, 1997.

————. *Zionism and the State of Israel: A Moral Inquiry*. London: Routledge, 1999.

Pugh, M., N. Cooper, and M. Turner, eds. *Whose Peace? Critical Perspectives on the Political Economy of Peacebuilding*. Houndmills, Basingstoke, UK: Palgrave Macmillan, 2008.

"Projected Mid-Year Population for Bethlehem Governorate by Locality 2017–2021." http://www.pcbs.gov.ps/Portals/_Rainbow/Documents/BethlehemE.html.

Raheb, Mitri. *Bethlehem Besieged: Stories of Hope in Times of Trouble*. Minneapolis: Fortress Press, 2004.

————. *Faith in the Face of Empire: The Bible through Palestinian Eyes*. Maryknoll, NY: Orbis Books, 2014.

————. *I Am a Palestinian Christian*. Minneapolis: Fortress Press, 1995.

————. "Jerusalem in the Age of Trump." In *Jerusalem: Religious, National and International Dimensions*. Ed. Mitri Raheb, 23–34. Bethlehem: Diyar, 2019.

Raheb, Mitri, ed. *The Biblical Text in the Context of Occupation: Towards a New Hermeneutics of Liberation*. Bethlehem: Diyar, 2012.

————. *The Invention of History: A Century of Interplay between*

Theology and Politics in Palestine. Bethlehem: Diyar, 2011.

Rantisi, Audeh G. *Blessed Are the Peacemakers: A Palestinian Christian in the Occupied West Bank*. Grand Rapids: Zondervan Books, 1990.

Robinson, Shira N. *Citizen Strangers: Palestinians and the Birth of Israel's Liberal Settler State*. Stanford, CA: Stanford University Press, 2013.

Rouhana, Nadim N. "Religious Claims and Nationalism in Zionism: Obscuring Settler Colonialism," in N. Rouhana and N. Shalhoub-Kevorkian, eds. *When Politics Are Sacralized: Comparative Perspectives on Religious Claims and Nationalism*. Cambridge: Cambridge University Press, 2021, 54. doi:10.1017/9781108768191.004.

Rouhana, Nadim N., and Areej Sabbagh-Khoury. "Settler-Colonial Citizenship: Conceptualizing the Relationship between Israel and Its Palestinian Citizens." *Settler Colonial Studies* 5, no. 3 (2015): 205–25.

Ruether, Rosemary Radford, and Herman J. Ruether. *The Wrath of Jonah: The Crisis of Religious Nationalism in the Israeli-Palestinian Conflict*. New York: HarperCollins, 1989.

Sabbagh-Khoury, Areej. "Tracing Settler Colonialism: A Genealogy of a Paradigm in the Sociology of Knowledge Production in Israel." *Politics & Society* 50, no. 1 (2021): 44.

Said, Edward W. *Orientalism*. New York: Vintage, 1979.

———. "Zionism from the Standpoint of Its Victims." *Social Text*, no. 1 (1979): 7–58.

Salaita, Steven. *Holy Land in Transit: Colonialism and the Quest for Canaan*. Syracuse, NY: Syracuse University Press, 2006.

———. *Inter/Nationalism: Decolonizing Native America and Palestine*. 3rd ed. Minneapolis: University of Minnesota Press, 2016.

Sand, Shlomo. *The Invention of the Jewish People*. London: Verso, 2009.

———. *The Invention of the Land of Israel*. London: Verso, 2012.

Sayegh, Fayez Abdullah. *Zionism: A Form of Racism and Racial*

Discrimination: Four Statements Made at the U.N. General Assembly. Office of the Permanent Observer of the Palestine Liberation Organization to the United Nations, 1976.

———. *Zionist Colonialism in Palestine.* Research Center, Palestine Liberation Organization, 1965.

Sayigh, Rosemary. "Oral History, Colonialist Dispossession, and the State: The Palestinian Case." *Settler Colonial Studies* 5, no. 3 (2015): 193–204.

Segovia, Fernando F. "Criticism in Critical Times: Reflections on Vision and Task." *Journal of Biblical Literature* 134, no. 1 (2015): 6.

———. "Engaging the Palestinian Theological-Critical Project of Liberation: A Critical Dialogue." In *The Biblical Text in the Context of Occupation: Towards a New Hermeneutics of Liberation.* Ed. Mitri Raheb, 29–80. Bethlehem: CreateSpace Independent Publishing Platform, 2012.

Sizer, Stephen. *Christian Zionism: Road Map to Armageddon?* Leicester, UK: Inter-Varsity, 2004.

Shihade, Magid. "Settler Colonialism and Conflict: The Israeli State and Its Palestinian Subjects." *Settler Colonial Studies* 2, no. 1 (2012): 108.

Slabodsky, S. *Decolonial Judaism: Triumphal Failures of Barbaric Thinking.* New York: Palgrave Macmillan, 2014.

Stasiulis, Daiva K., and Nira Yuval-Davis, eds. *Unsettling Settler Societies: Articulations of Gender, Race, Ethnicity and Class.* London: SAGE Publications, 1995.

Sugirtharajah, R. S. *Exploring Postcolonial Biblical Criticism History, Method, Practice.* Chichester, UK2012.

Tarazi, Paul Nadim. *Land and Covenant.* London: OCABS Press, 2009.

Thompson, Derek. "Three Decades Ago, America Lost Its Religion. Why?" *The Atlantic*, September 26, 2019. https://www.theatlantic.com/ideas/archive/2019/09/atheism-fastest-growing-religion-us/598843/.

Thompson, Thomas. *Early History of the Israelite People: From the Written & Archaeological Sources*. Leiden, the Netherlands: Brill Academic Publishers, 1841.

Tinker, George E. *Missionary Conquest: The Gospel and Native American Cultural Genocide*. Minneapolis: Fortress Press, 1993.

Trump, Donald J. "Proclamation on Jerusalem as the Capital of the State of Israel." https://trumpwhitehouse.archives.gov/briefings-statements/president-donald-j-trumps-proclamation-jerusalem-capital-state-israel/. December 6, 2017.

—————. "Proclamation on Recognizing the Golan Heights as Part of the State of Israel." https://trumpwhitehouse.archives.gov/presidential-actions/proclamation-recognizing-golan-heights-part-state-israel/. March 25, 2019.

Tubb, Jonathan N. *Canaanites*. Illustrated ed. Norman: University of Oklahoma Press, 1999.

Turner, Mandy. "Completing the Circle: Peacebuilding as Colonial Practice in the Occupied Palestinian Territory." *International Peacekeeping* 19, no. 4 (2012): 492–507.

—————. "Peacebuilding as Counterinsurgency in the Occupied Palestinian Territory." *Review of International Studies* 41, no. 1 (2015): 1–26.

UNESCO World Heritage Centre. "Palestine: Land of Olives and Vines—Cultural Landscape of Southern Jerusalem, Battir." https://whc.unesco.org/en/list/1492/.

Veracini, Lorenzo. *Israel and Settler Society*. London: Pluto Press, 2006.

—————. *Settler Colonialism: A Theoretical Overview*. Houndmills, Basingstoke, UK: Palgrave Macmillan, 2010.

—————. "The Other Shift: Settler Colonialism, Israel, and the Occupation." *Journal of Palestine Studies* 42, no. 2 (2013): 26–42.

—————. *The Settler Colonial Present*. Houndmills, Basingstoke, UK: Palgrave Macmillan, 2015.

————. "What Can Settler Colonial Studies Offer to an Interpretation of the Conflict in Israel–Palestine?" *Settler Colonial Studies* 5, no. 3 (2015): 268–71.

Warrior, Robert Allen. "A North American Perspective: Canaanites, Cowboys, and Indians." In *Voices from the Margin: Interpreting the Bible in the Third World.* Ed. R. S. Sugirtharajah, 25th Anniversary ed., 235–41. Maryknoll, NY: Orbis Books, 2016.

West, Jim, and James G. Crossley. *History, Politics and the Bible from the Iron Age to the Media Age: Essays in Honour of Keith W. Whitelam.* London: Bloomsbury T&T Clark, 2017.

Whitelam, Keith W. *The Invention of Ancient Israel: The Silencing of Palestinian History.* London: Routledge, 1996.

Wolfe, Patrick. "Settler Colonialism and the Elimination of the Native." *Journal of Genocide Research* 8, no. 4 (2006): 387–409.

————. *Settler Colonialism and the Transformation of Anthropology: The Politics and Poetics of an Ethnograph Event.* London: Continuum, 1999.

Younan, Munib. *Our Shared Witness: A Voice for Justice and Reconciliation.* Minneapolis: Lutheran University Press, 2012.

————. *Witnessing for Peace: In Jerusalem and the World.* Minneapolis: Fortress Press, 2003.

Zureik, Elia. *Israel's Colonial Project in Palestine: Brutal Pursuit.* London: Routledge, 2015.

————. *The Palestinians in Israel: A Study in Internal Colonialism.* London: Routledge & K. Paul, 1979.

Index